AFTERSHOCK

The Quake on Everest and One Man's Quest

Jules Mountain

Published in 2017
by Eye Books
29A Barrow Street
Much Wenlock
Shropshire
TF13 6EN
www.eye-books.com

ISBN: 978-1-78563-501-4

British Library Cataloguing in Publication Data
A catalogue record for this book is available from the British Library

Printed by CPI Group (UK) Ltd, Croydon CR0 4YY

Contents

The avalanche and the big C

My head throbs from the festivities of the night before. Alcohol is not a good idea at altitude, but we were dancing and drinking into the early hours with very little oxygen, so I am enjoying a quiet rest day.

I'm lying in my 'coffin' – my minute tent at Everest Base Camp. The canvas is about half a metre above my face, and my two kit bags are squeezed in next to me. It's -2°C. My breath rises from my mouth like small plumes of smoke as I try to catch a midday nap.

My feet are tucked in the end of my sleeping bag; my eyes are shut. The sun is shining in through the tent lining – a day like any other I've experienced in the five weeks I've been here.

Suddenly and without warning, the ground I am lying on abruptly moves half a metre to the left.

I open my eyes with a start. What on earth? Did that really happen? Did the entire earth just shift beneath me? Or was it last night's whisky?

Again, I feel the earth move. The ground underneath me lifts me up half a metre, as if something is pushing into my back, before suddenly shunting to the right. What the hell's happening? I am lying on a glacier of 100 tons of ice – nothing could move that!

I heave myself up out of my sleeping bag; rip the tent zip open. The snow in front of me, calm and serene, blissfully unaware of the plans the mountain has in store for it, clings to me as I half-crawl out and stand upright.

I see Donat and Iwan just in front of me, staring up at Pumori as if hypnotised. Usually, with Everest looming so majestically overhead, there is little reason to look at the Goliath's smaller sister, but right now... Careering down Mount Pumori is the biggest avalanche I have ever seen. Coming right at us...

The entire sky is filled with a giant, cascading wall of white. A beautiful and deadly collision of debris – rocks, ice and white dust – and all of it heading straight for me.

It rolls, turns, tumbles every which way, billowing right and left and everywhere, as it surges invincibly on down the mountain.

From ground to sky there is nothing else; just this wall of whiteness thundering towards us, oblivious of all in its path, full of heartless violence.

Everything is gone – nothing exists in the world, but this...

Crikey!... This is it – I'm dead! I'm dead!

There is nothing I can do but accept that I am about to be swept away forever by an avalanche. After all the near misses and close calls of my life, after all the lucky escapes from hospital, I must exit here, thousands of miles from my loved ones.

My daughters, my girlfriend, my family in England drift into my mind; time seems to be slowing infinitely to allow me to think about them all, one last time. It feels as if 15 minutes have passed since I emerged from my tent, but it's actually only a few seconds.

I look down. I'm not even wearing boots; just socks on my half-frozen feet. Could I run? I glance over my shoulder.

Donat and Iwan have thrown themselves behind a two-foot rocky outcrop, but I don't have time to get there.

Running is out of the question. The avalanche is hurtling towards me at 150 kilometres an hour, and the ground is an obstacle course of rocks, guide ropes and ice. I am sure to trip. And anyway, where to run? I think of the icy lake just behind me on the glacier – what if the avalanche throws me in?

I have to get down. Now.

I dive headfirst into my tent, and hit the floor, burrowing my head into the ground.

The avalanche is on me, all around and on top of me.

I am being buried alive in snow.

* * * * *

How on earth had I come to such a pass? What was I doing on Everest in the first place?

My original goal in life was to build and sell a company, and I achieved that in 2005, when I sold my management consultancy business to a French firm. I then went on to build another consultancy business and sell that in 2007, just before the crash, so it seemed I was doubly lucky, but that wasn't the only thing going on in my life...

Just before selling my second business I found a lump on my head, behind my ear. I was told there was an 80% chance it was a benign lump. In other words, a harmless growth. Of course I am not an 80% guy; I am a 20% guy, and no, it was not a benign lump – it was a tumour. I had cancer – the big C. It's like a steam train hitting you – your world stops.

And not just any cancer; it was in my head. If it had been in my leg or arm it could be cut off, but you can't exactly cut your head off – it's a little bit self-defeating. And just when I was trying to sell my business.

I spent the next two weeks in and out of hospital, having scans and tests, and a great big needle stuck into my head, just behind my ear, with no anaesthetic.

After a painfully long and nerve-wracking week, during which I tried very hard to focus on the consultancy business and not to think about the lump, I went back for the results. As I walked in I saw the consultant's face looking up at me sympathetically. Before he had even opened his mouth, I knew – it was cancer. He said it could be one of two types; one was treatable, the other was not good. When he said "not good", I didn't realise that, in consultant speak, this means you will be dead in a matter of weeks. Unfortunately, the biopsy did not identify which one it was, so he recommended they operate on me immediately.

On top of selling the management consultancy business, I was also moving house that weekend. I decided I should move house anyway. Otherwise I might never live in my new home at all. So the operation was planned for the next Tuesday.

I came out of the consultant's office feeling very, very sick.

The move was a blessing in disguise, as it kept me busy all weekend, hefting boxes with the removal men and making beds and getting the kitchen up and running.

When Monday came I was very nervous. I went into the office as usual and told the staff I was having an operation, and that I wouldn't be in for the next week, thinking to myself that I might never be back there at all.

I went into hospital early on Tuesday morning after a sleepless night. The consultant told me it was to be a seven-hour operation, in which they would remove the parotid gland, and all the lymph nodes around the gland and further down my neck. And then he hit me with it: "We may have to remove your voice box. Please sign this consent form."

I duly signed, not knowing, if I came round at all, whether I would be able to speak. I hate going under, as I feel I am losing control, and I am a control freak.

During the operation they severed all the nerves in the left side of my face, causing that side of my face to drop and nothing to work normally.

When I came round, I was high as a kite on whatever they'd given me, and very, very sleepy, but I *could* talk. Thank goodness.

I looked truly terrible, as if someone had slid the whole of the left side of my face downwards. I couldn't find the parts of that side of my face; my brain didn't know where they were because all the nerve endings had been severed and re-joined in a random pattern. I had an itch on the top of my ear, but my hand couldn't find the top of my ear – it was really weird, as if the left-hand side of my face was not mine but somebody else's.

My brother, Rick, came to see me the next day. He is my rock and we are very close. We discuss all our issues together. I wanted to sit up in bed to try to feel normal, but my brain didn't know what was going on. I was in intense pain, even with the painkillers, and I couldn't speak properly because I couldn't move the left side of my mouth, so I slurred my words. But we chatted.

Then I wanted to get out of bed for a pee. My brother called the nurse and she helped me slowly to my feet.

I was like a 100-year-old man as I hobbled to the loo. The nurse had to help me pee (no room for dignity). I was horrified when I caught a glimpse of my face in the mirror. I looked like Quasimodo.

I shuffled back over to the bed and very slowly sat in the armchair next to it. I was desperate to feel normal. I sat for the next three hours chatting to Rick. My head was spinning, trying to compute what had gone on in the past 24 hours. I was in a lot of pain, but at the same time, I had a numb, out-of-body feeling.

Suddenly, I started to feel very poorly. I asked Rick to help me get back into bed.

As he did so, I could feel my heart racing. "I feel really ill. Get the nurse, get the nurse!"

My brother's face showed total panic. He looked at me again and then dashed for the door, screaming, "NURSE! NURSE!

MY BROTHER! NURSE!"

She came running in and immediately pressed the red button behind me. It was the crash team button... Oh shit, this wasn't going to be good.

Next thing, a doctor comes running in, followed by a team of two with a trolley of equipment, and on top I could see the defibrillator. Bloody hell, I'd survived the op but now I was going to die the day after.

My heart was racing and my chest felt very, very tight, as if I had a car on top of me. I was sure I was having a heart attack – not uncommon after a general anaesthetic and a lengthy operation.

"We may have to open you up so that I can massage your heart." WHAT?! "It's a messy procedure and we will have to cut your sternum."

Jeepers. My heart raced even faster. This was it. I was going to die.

While the doctor was telling me this, the others were ripping off my pyjamas and sticking pads all over my chest. If I hadn't been having a heart attack, this was enough to bring one on.

The doctor was shouting at the team as they stuck a tube down my throat, to stop me from choking when they cut me open. He then rolled me on to my side and shoved the largest needle you have ever seen into my backside. It made the biopsy needle look wimpy. My heart was racing so fast I thought it would come out of my chest. They then rolled me back and put an oxygen mask on me and started an IV drip. I could feel myself drifting.

The doctor was looking into my eyes, but I was fading fast. I tried to find my brother. I was mumbling, "Rick, Rick, Rick". He took my hand and I drifted off.

I awoke some time later to a lot of concerned faces staring down at me. I had gone into anaphylactic shock as a result of the operation, and nearly died.

"Am I ok?" I mumbled through the oxygen mask.

"You are for now. We're going to monitor you closely," said the doctor.

"Rick, don't leave me, please, please, don't leave me, I don't want to die alone tonight."

"I won't leave you". They brought a camp bed in and Rick slept right next to me, holding my hand all night.

In the morning, the consultant came. "I heard we had a bit of an incident last night."

"Yes, we did, but please let me go home." So they discharged me that afternoon and my brother drove me home very, very slowly. Every speed bump and pothole hurt like hell.

This experience gave me the belief that you have to live every day as if it's your last.

Over the next five months, I had gruelling chemotherapy, all my hair fell out and some of my veins collapsed. I was determined to prove to myself that I was no less of a man, that anything I could do before I could still do now, and that I could get back to the same level of physical fitness. What I needed was a physical challenge to prove this, and the more challenging, the more I would prove it to myself.

You never feel more alive than when you're close to death!

From days on Mont Blanc to dreams of Everest

The wind buffeted us wildly as we stepped out on to the knife-edged ridge. We checked our harnesses one last time before we began the 150-metre crossing. People had been known to lose their lives on this treacherous arête, plummeting hundreds of metres before smashing on to the rocks below.

I knelt down, checked my crampons. The metal gleamed in the sunlight like precious silver. I tightened them – better to be safe, I thought.

They're strange things, crampons (basically metal spikes that strap to the bottom of your climbing boots); they make my feet feel alien, cumbersome. They always remind me of something from a James Bond film – that bad guy with the poison-tipped knife in his shoe.

I could feel the wind blowing against my face, yet also the lack of oxygen in the air. I took a deep breath.

We edged tentatively along, the rope tied between us giving just enough slack. I could feel a bead of sweat on my temple.

I looked up. The scenery was magnificent: a sprawling array of snow-covered mountains as far as the eye could see, the purity of their snow-capped peaks contrasting vividly with a seamlessly blue sky.

No time for that now. I could appreciate the beauty when I got back – when I was safe.

Step by step, we inched closer to the plateau at the far end.

I gripped my ice axe tightly, ready at a second's notice to dig it into the ground and arrest a fall, if either Fred or I tumbled.

Fred was about five metres ahead of me. The wind was howling, and he huddled against it in his protective clothing, advancing cautiously.

I trusted Fred; he was a great guy. There are very few people in the world that I trust enough to be roped to – after all I'm 15 stone, and if I fell, Fred would have to hold me – a six-foot-three, 95-kilo guy takes some holding.

But...there was still that nagging doubt. If I fell, if I failed to arrest myself with my axe, would he react in time? Would his mind be quick enough, would he jump off the other side of the ridge to counterbalance me? That's a tall order when it comes to it.

I didn't know – there was only one way of knowing, and I didn't much fancy taking that bet.

We shuffled onwards towards our goal, each locked in our own thoughts, eyes down, focused on where we were putting our feet.

With each step, I pulled my foot free, fighting against the suction of the snow, and wedged the toes of the crampon a step ahead. I took care to avoid the sharp edges of the crampon – I'd lost many a pair of salopettes (trousers) to these lethal things.

Next time I looked up, unexpectedly I saw we had arrived; I breathed out heavily, as if I'd been holding my breath the whole way across.

As we unroped, I took a second to appreciate the scenery. Not many people would be able to witness this first hand – I knew I was lucky, so it felt a shame not to be able to stay there for longer.

Time was marching on, though. And so must we.

We re-roped on a longer reach as we began descending from the smaller plateau to the Vallée Blanche, high above Chamonix. Up near the top of Mont Blanc, alone, on foot in thick snow, we might as well have been 1,000 miles away from anywhere. We trudged on, the snow crunching under our feet with every step as the crampons went in.

All the time, I kept my eyes peeled for hairline cracks in the snow; that telltale sign that indicates a crevasse.

If I missed one and stepped onto the thin, breakable crust of snow that covered it, I would be swallowed whole by the darkness. If Fred could not arrest me, I'd be lost to the depths in less than a second.

As we carried on down into the valley, the wind dropped, and it turned into a beautiful day. The sun was beating down on us as we trudged on, sweating in our climbing clothes.

Below us, highlighted by sunlight, we could see the vast crevasses. Each one, a potential tomb.

We rounded a corner and stopped, shielding our eyes as we looked up the valley. Ahead of us, we could see it at last; our final destination.

The abandoned hut, close to the newer Refuge des Cosmiques, sitting atop a tiny outcrop, small and insignificant against the backdrop of the Mont Blanc massif.

* * * * *

I was in the Alps for the Ski Club of Great Britain – as a Leader, which meant I flew out to France every couple of months and acted as a ski guide for the club members. In the evenings, I would go to the Office bar, which was run by a lively New Zealander called Dave.

On this particular evening, I found myself chatting with Dave and a friend of his, whom I immediately recognised. He was well known in the area, and in the climbing world generally. Soon the conversation turned to climbing.

"What have you done?" he asked me.

An odd question, slightly forward, I thought. He was a straight-to-the-point kind of guy.

"I've climbed Mont Blanc," I said. "I've done a few other things, but I wouldn't say I'm a great mountaineer or anything."

He pondered this for a while. He seemed to be assessing me, and he knew I was a ski club guide.

"I've got a space on an expedition in a couple of months," he said, matter-of-factly.

My interest was piqued. This could be a good adventure, I thought – would it be the Eiger, Matterhorn, Jungfrau?

"Where?"

"Everest."

"*Everest?*"

That moment was intensely exhilarating. Everest... Actual Everest, *the* actual Everest. The real thing. I'm in the pub in Chamonix having a few beers, this guy walks in and all of a sudden...I have a chance to go to Everest! Blow me over with another pint of beer!

He explained that the expedition was leaving in late March, so I would have only three weeks to prepare. He seemed so casual about the whole thing – about *Everest*.

My thrill at the opportunity was laced with nervousness, a tingling apprehension.

I could have walked away at that point, thanked him for the opportunity and found an excuse not to go. "It's too soon," I could have said. "My kids...the equipment...the expenses...the training..."

Here it was, though, laid out for me on a plate; an opportunity to do something I'd always wanted to do. An opportunity I might never see again. Could I refuse? Did I even have a choice?

Essentially, there are two types of people in the world – those who make excuses, and those who throw caution to the wind and go for it. Every time a crazy opportunity like this turns up I remind myself of this, and it's got me into trouble on a number of occasions.

I knew in my heart that I wanted to go, but my kids? We agreed to meet in London two weeks later, once I had had a chance to think things through. And that was that.

In five or six weeks, I thought, I could be heading off for the adventure of a lifetime – little realising at the time what kind of adventure it would actually be.

It took two days of soul-searching to come to a conclusion. Two days of mulling the whole thing over and thinking of all the reasons why I shouldn't go.

I didn't mention it to anyone during that time; I didn't want anyone else's opinions or negativity influencing my decision. I wanted to get the whole thing straight in my own mind and to be able to rationalise it in my own head before talking it over with anyone else.

Two days later, I'd committed.

Everest.

* * * * *

It was three weeks later and I was back in the Alps. The ski clubbers had left on the Sunday and I had a free day on Monday before I flew home.

I had convinced Fred to help me practise for Everest; we were going to try out all the techniques I would need up there. We would do ice axe arrests (falling down a steep slope and jumping on your axe to stop yourself – crazy, really, because you can puncture yourself with the axe, but very useful if you do fall, and get it right, and manage to stop), and climbing with a jumar. (This is a device you attach to a static rope that has been put into the rock face in advance and the jumar will slide forwards but not backwards down the rope. The jumar is then attached via a cord to your harness so if you fall you don't slide down the slope – a rather clever piece of kit.)

I also wanted to try out my new Everest summit boots. These are specially made for Everest and manufactured as three boots in one – the waterproof outer liner, the middle foil lining to keep the heat from evaporating from my feet, and the inner layer to keep my feet comfortable, padded and warm. They are built to withstand -40°C at the summit of Everest.

I'd visited Snell Sports in Chamonix, one of the few places in Europe to sell these boots. It had been a pretty big deal for me, buying them; it made the whole thing seem more real, and symbolised my commitment to the project.

They were hefty things, reaching up almost to my knees. They had a bright red strip from the toe to the top, flanked by yellow on either side. 'Everest Summit' was written on the side.

When Sir Edmund Hillary first conquered Everest in 1953, 31 companies were involved in the manufacture of his summit boots. Mine were made by just one – Millet – but developments in mountain clothing in the past 60 years have been considerable. I would likely be carrying half the weight in equipment, but have twice the protection.

The weather in the Alps was absolutely perfect for what I wanted to do; it was blowing a gale, dark clouds dotted the sky; visibility was minimal. Exactly what I needed to try out my new equipment, and to prove to myself that if things turned nasty on Everest, I could take it.

Fred and I made our way to that ridge again, but this time, the gale felt strong enough to blow us away. I remembered a story I'd heard of a skier and a snowboarder, from the previous season. They came up on the Aiguille du Midi cable car to Mont Blanc, to 3,800m at the end of the day, to ski the Vallée Blanche back down to Chamonix. This is a common off-piste ski route, but treacherous, because it is full of crevasses.

As they crossed the thin ridge to the small plateau, the weather turned, the fog came in – it can turn very quickly up there – so they sensibly decided to make their way back along the ridge to the cable car station.

The skier made it back to the station and turned to welcome his friend, and to laugh about what fools they had been to come out in the first place...only, his friend wasn't there.

He must have just slowed up for some reason, the skier assumed, preparing himself to bunk down for the night. The cable car would not be running in that weather; they would have to rough it.

Five minutes passed.

The skier started to become worried.

Ten minutes passed.

He looked out over the ridge and tried to pick out any shapes, but all he could see was snow blasting across his face. All he could hear was the howling of the wind.

Thirty minutes passed.

He contacted the emergency services, who informed him there was nothing they could do. He would have to wait, the wind was too strong to run the cable car, the helicopters couldn't fly in such weather. He said his friend was missing, but they said he'd have to wait.

He resigned himself for what would be an uncomfortable night's sleep, in more ways than one.

The emergency services arrived at dawn.

It wasn't long before they found the snowboarder, 300 metres below the Aiguille du Midi, smashed to pieces on sharp rocks. His snowboard, acting like a sail, must have pulled him off the ridge and dropped him down below, his shrieks of fear lost in the howling wind.

A horrible way to die – and he would have been very aware that he was going to die. He would have known what was happening; he would have had time to consider his imminent and gruesome death, going like a rocket before he hit the rocks at the bottom of the mountain.

I didn't want to become another horror story like that.

I'd had skiing accidents, of course – every skier pays for his passion with a few cuts and bruises. Mine included broken ribs on three occasions, a broken leg, two broken arms, a broken thumb and a dislocated arm (excruciatingly painful). The bunch of mates I ski with annually always try to guess whose turn it is to get injured each year. I've had more than my fair share of hits.

I was bent double, almost on my hands and knees, Fred just a blurry silhouette ahead of me. I clutched my ice axe, stabbing the tip into the snow with every step. My whole focus was keeping myself on the ridge, taking the next step.

We arrived at the end of the ridge, exhausted, struggling for breath in the thin air.

I heard Fred shout at me from what seemed a million miles

away.

"Jules!" he shouted. "We don't want to do this – I think we should go down!"

But this was what I wanted; I wanted to practise in the most terribly adverse conditions. I wanted the mountain to chuck everything it had at me.

I stood, arms out to the heavens, the elements doing their best to sweep me off the mountain.

"Come on!" I shouted. "Come on you mother! Come and get me! Give me your best shot!"

I screamed like some crazy guy (doing Everest *is* crazy), my yells whipped away by the thrashing wind. Fred must have thought I was bonkers, standing on a mountaintop, screaming for more. The extreme nature of the situation made me feel all the more alive, all the more invigorated.

We made it to the hut, pushed the heavy door closed and stopped for a drink and some chocolate. The hut was a ramshackle affair, no more than three metres square, with the wind ripping through the gaps in its wooden planking like something from an old Western movie. Its high-pitched whistling dizzied the senses.

On either side of the small room were rudimentary bunks, barely more than planks of wood. The building was basically a wooden shack, perched precariously on the mountain.

I wondered with amazement at the effort it would have taken to get the building materials up there in the first place. The wood was heavy-duty timber – it would survive hundreds of winters – but it would have been lugged up by hand. There were no cable cars in those days.

"Jules," Fred said, wringing water from his sodden gloves, "it's not safe."

I knew that – of course it wasn't safe, but I wasn't going to be safe on Everest either. I wanted to be prepared; I wanted to know how I was going to react if the situation became desperate.

While Fred was under-prepared for this kind of weather, I was feeling more than toasty. The new equipment I'd purchased for Everest was working a treat – I could have stayed up there all day.

I convinced Fred that we'd be fine, that I needed the practice in these conditions. Begrudgingly, he agreed to carry on, pulling his gloves back on and sighing. Of course, for me, the adrenalin was pumping like mad – for Fred, the whole thing was probably totally miserable.

I think he thought I was an absolute nutter.

We left the hut, struggling with the heavy door against the wind, and made our way towards the bottom of the Cosmique Arrêt. We climbed a short way up the Arrêt, and attached a rope for me to practise with my jumar and descender.

Fred sheltered behind an old stone hut – the remnants of an old cable car hut – he curled himself up in a ball, not talking much, focusing on keeping warm. The wind and snow sailed around us viciously.

The incline was at about 50 degrees. Again and again, I gripped the fixed rope and slid my jumar, hauling myself up afterwards. My thick gloves made it hard to operate the equipment, and of course you never remove your gloves, as frostbite quickly sets in. An army friend of mine told me it was a court-martial offence to remove your gloves in snowy conditions without first attaching them to a safety cord – seems a bit severe, but I get it.

On reaching the top, I would change to my descender (it looks like a figure of eight, and you loop the rope through it to create friction to slow your descent) and lower myself back down again, and then I would do it all over again. All of it in the howling, freezing wind. Of course, on Everest I would be wearing three pairs of gloves – but it was hard enough operating the equipment with just one pair.

"Have you had enough yet?" Fred yelled from his sheltered position each time I returned to the bottom.

"No, no!" I shouted above the wind, "I want to do more!"

The wind was howling around my face, whipping up the loose snow; I could feel my nose getting colder and colder.

I gripped the jumar, pulling myself up the rope again. I reached the top, took a few seconds to recover, then went back down again.

"Have you had enough yet?"

There was desperation in Fred's voice. I felt sorry for him, under-prepared, having been dragged up a freezing cold mountain to watch some crazed Englishman pull himself up and down a cliff.

"Not yet!"

I had my hood up and goggles on, all my layers on, all the protective gear I was going to need for Everest. Still, white dots began forming on my nose from the cold – the start of frostbite.

I pulled myself up the rope again.

After the fifth time, I was entirely exhausted and out of breath. I was panting like a dog on a hot summer's day – the tank was nearly empty. In spite of the freezing cold, I was hot – the insulating layers of my clothing were doing a great job at keeping the heat in, to the point that I was very cosy.

Fred was not so warm.

I looked at him, huddled for warmth behind the derelict remains of a cable car station. He cut a very lonely figure there, waiting for me to finish.

"I need to practise ice axe arrests," I yelled at Fred, struggling to make myself heard against the wind.

He nodded, screwing up his face like a schoolboy being forced to do something he doesn't want to.

We headed back along the treacherous ridge, towards the top of the Aiguille du Midi, the perfect location to practise.

"Ok, Jules, now you jump off," said Fred. Was that a twang of sick glee masked within his French accent?

We're at nearly 4,000m, at the top of a steep incline, and Fred is telling me to jump off!

I sat down on the edge, ice axe clutched at the ready. I gently pushed myself off the side, like a timorous child on a slide.

I soon gained speed on the icy snow. I turned on my side, dug my axe into the snow, praying that it would bite, that I wouldn't continue my descent to whatever lay below

The axe bit, I stopped moving with a jerk.

I let out a relieved sigh and used my crampons to make my way back up to Fred.

"That was rubbish!" he yelled, laughing through frozen cheeks. "You must jump!"

I was starting to think Fred might be getting his own back. I prepped myself to go again, steadying myself to jump off the mountainside.

Suddenly, out of nowhere, I received a sharp shove in the back, causing me to fly off the side of the mountain.

I tumbled, turning in the cascading snow as I plummeted downwards.

I remembered the axe – the axe!

Instinct took over; I jerked myself onto my side, smashing the axe into the snow to my left.

The axe bit, I gripped with all that I had – if it slipped, I was toast.

As suddenly as I had started, I stopped dead. Everything instantly felt very quiet and still as I clung to the axe, hanging over the edge of the ridge.

Meanwhile, safely on the ridge, Fred was laughing. He *was* getting his own back.

In a sick way, Fred had done me a favour. On Everest, if the shit hit the fan, I wouldn't be expecting it – there would be no time for me to prepare myself mentally. The sharp push was what I needed to know that I could cope.

I got back up to Fred. "Let's head back and I'll buy you dinner," I shouted. I'd had enough close shaves for one day.

I think he would have smiled if his face hadn't been so cold.

It had been good practice. I felt better prepared for Everest, more ready for what the beast would throw at me. I knew the conditions weren't going to be exactly the same. For one thing, there wouldn't be emergency help so close at hand, or as much oxygen, but I felt slightly more confident that I could do it.

I thought of myself on the summit of Everest, looking out across the world. I would be, for one brief moment, the highest 'Mountain' on the planet.

Leaving loved ones

I woke with a jolt, struggling to focus my eyes in the darkness – where was I? What was that noise?

"You fell asleep!" said a soft voice.

My eyes finally adjusted and brought the room into focus. In front of me, the television was playing the American cartoon we had been watching when I nodded off.

I looked down at the two faces beaming up at me from either side. Steph (12), and Lizzie (9) – my girls. We were snuggled up on the sofa together, wrapped in a thick duvet.

They giggled. I smiled down at them, pulling them closer. I wanted to remember that moment.

Whenever I had time with my girls it was special – I was always acutely aware of that. They had to share their time between my house and their mother's, which must be tough on them. Every day that I woke up without them nearby, my heart broke ever so slightly; it was far from the perfect situation, but we had to make it work, as many families do.

The previous evening I had sat the girls down and told them I was going to try to climb Everest. I had practised what I was going to say a million times, but the real thing is always harder.

"Girls, Dad's got something to tell you."

This piqued their curiosity – they looked up quizzically, with narrowed eyes. They always seemed to know when something was serious.

"Dad's going on a great trip soon," I said. I was very eager to be positive about the whole thing. "I'm going to try to climb Everest."

I thought I saw a tear well up in Lizzie's eye. I moved on quickly.

"Which means I'm going to be away for a while. You won't see me – you'll be staying with your mum. I'm going to text you and email you lots, and we'll talk on the phone. I'll come back with lots of great stories for you. It's a great honour to be invited on the expedition, that they think I am worthy of being in their team. It's a well-equipped expedition, and we will be very careful."

Naturally, they had a few questions. We discussed Everest and Nepal for a bit. I explained that professionals were running the trip, and that they would help me stay safe.

I promised to bring them back some presents from Nepal – this excited them.

And that was pretty much that. Everest wasn't mentioned again that evening.

As we sat on the sofa, with *Hoodwinked* playing in the background, I thought about how much I was going to miss them.

Two months.

This would be, by far, the longest I had spent away from my two girls.

One question kept coming back to trouble me: why was I doing this?

Why was I – a father of two – risking my life to climb a mountain? I couldn't quite reach an answer that made sense to me, but still the urge to go was overwhelming.

I tried to put these thoughts out of my mind, to focus on the present, on my last few hours with the girls before my adventure began. After the film, I tucked them up in bed; we had a cuddle and I kissed them goodnight.

They were excited about what I was going to do. I thought I noticed an extra gleam of pride in their eyes as I told them I loved them and wished them goodnight.

The following day, Lizzie rushed off to school, full of excitement. She told all her school friends, 'Dad's going to climb Everest'. Although she didn't want me to go, I think she was actually quite proud of me.

The day after, I went to watch her play netball at school. As the match finished, a gaggle of her friends rushed up.

"Lizzie says you're going to climb Everest – you're not, are you?" one of them said, in that way that only children can.

"I'm going to attempt to climb Everest," I said.

The whole thing amazed the kids; the idea that one of the dads they knew was going to attempt to climb Everest astounded them.

I knew my daughters were proud of me, and this, along with love, is all a father ever really wants.

* * * * *

My girlfriend Vicky took time off work to give me a lift to the airport. This was particularly nice because it delayed the inevitable; the moment I left Vicky I was going to be on my own for two months...a lonely two months.

She gave me some Easter chocolates and an apple strudel to eat on the plane. The chocolates I saved until Kathmandu.

We lugged the heavy bags on to the trolley from the boot of the car – two massive kit bags, full to the brim with climbing equipment, survival gear, everything I would need to stay alive.

My final bag, my rucksack, was smaller, containing my non-climbing equipment and electrical items such as my laptop, phone and solar charger.

I had set up a blog for the trip, in order to keep my friends and family updated on my adventures – as well as for something to do in my down time.

I had heard that internet connections at Everest Base Camp are not good, so updating a live blog was out of the question. I had arranged to send a daily email with a short update and a couple of photos to Freecom, a company that had agreed to support me. They would then update the text and photos on the live blog.

The blog was also intended to keep those sponsoring my trip for charity informed of my progress and connected to my story.

A few years ago, I was diagnosed with non-Hodgkins lymphoma. Shortly afterwards, my father was diagnosed with the same condition. Although we both ultimately recovered, it was a long and difficult journey. I feel heavily indebted to the staff at University College London Hospital (UCLH) for the remarkable support they gave us during that tough time.

So, as a token of my immense gratitude, I wanted to support the UCLH Leukaemia and Lymphoma Cancer Unit, their charity arm. I hoped the sponsorship donations might enable them to purchase a piece of equipment that would aid in the earlier detection of cancer, and potentially save lives.

I slung the smaller backpack on my back, kissed Vicky goodbye and thanked her again for all she had done to help me in the run-up to my departure.

As I pushed my trolley into the airport, I felt I was taking my first real steps on the road towards the top of the world.

Some while later, my plane took off. Seven hours to Doha. A three-hour stopover and then five more hours to Kathmandu...

There was no turning back.

Joining the expedition

Twelve long hours and many films later, the plane began its final descent into Tribhuvan Airport.

After disembarking, I collected my luggage and made my way through to arrivals. I'm not sure what I was expecting – some sort of welcome party, someone to meet me...something.

There was nobody there.

It is quite a complicated process, landing in Nepal. You have to queue for a $100 visa as soon as you arrive, with a wait of nearly an hour.

But no matter, I was in Nepal. I was excited, apprehensive, nervous, all at the same time.

The airport had a similar feel to the one I had landed at in Bangkok, many years before. It was an old brick building with no plaster. The whole airport had an ambience of the 1970s, with an odd, lingering sweaty smell in the air. My excitement washed all of that away – this was Kathmandu; Everest was on the doorstep.

I took a taxi to the Hyatt Regency. This was our Kathmandu expedition base for the next couple of days. Here our equipment would be checked, we would meet our fellow climbers and get organised.

I spent the 15-minute taxi ride staring out of the window, taking in the sights and sounds of this new, alien place.

The city was a mêlée of cars and mopeds; the sound of their horns filled the streets. The traffic regulations of Britain seemed a very long way away, with vehicles fighting each other for space on the narrow roads.

There seemed to be no real system in place, but everything felt so chaotically vibrant and alive – it was a spectacle to behold. A motorbike sped past, overburdened with huge sacks strapped to the back. I could hardly see the driver. With impressive skill, he shimmied through the traffic, barely ever slowing, tooting his horn whenever a car or pedestrian got in his way. I noticed that all the motorbikes had three bull bars bolted onto the front, to protect the drivers from all the no-doubt frequent collisions.

The façade of the five-star Hyatt was spectacular, combining Western and Nepalese architecture to stunning effect. Two small pagodas flanked the entrance to the building.

The contrast between the bustling streets of Kathmandu and the serene stillness of the Hyatt Regency grounds was staggering. It was like stepping into a beautifully calm oasis, surrounded on all sides by the hustle and bustle of Kathmandu city.

I made my way into the lobby, passing through a large set of wooden doors covered in small golden domes.

The lobby was a large, open space, with a dipped central area dominated by 12 large stone sculptures, each depicting a famous Nepalese landmark. There was the Boudhanath, the large *stupa* on the outskirts of the city, and the architectural wonder that is Swayambhunath, full of holy monkeys. Although beautiful in their own rights, these were not what I had come to see.

I had come to see the most beautiful landmark of them all; one that no man had a hand in creating.

I didn't know it at the time, but some of the historic buildings I was looking at were very close to the end of their lives. By the time I returned here, six weeks later, they would be reduced to rubble and ash.

I was greeted at reception and escorted to my room.

Again, I was hit by that odd sensation – what now?

I rang the expedition leader's room number, to let him know that I had arrived.

"Hello?" A female voice answered the call.

"Hi," I said, "it's Jules Mountain here. I just thought I should let you know that I've arrived at the hotel."

There was a pause. Had I called the right number? What if I wasn't on the list? What if I'd come all this way only to hear them apologise and say that they didn't have any paperwork for me and that I'd have to go home.

"Jules...yes, Jules, hi," the voice said. I was more relieved than I ought to have been.

She explained she was the expedition leader's partner, and that he was not currently in.

"Relax," she said. "Take it easy. We're going to check everything during the next two days and make sure everyone has all the vital equipment they need for the expedition."

She told me there was an expedition briefing that evening, and that we were due to meet in the bar at six o'clock. She would introduce me to everybody then, and we would be given important information about our summit attempt.

I thanked her and hung up. It was becoming more and more real by the minute.

I sent a text to Vicky and the girls, to let them know I had arrived safely, before showering and changing.

At six o'clock, I made my way down to the bar. I knew no one on the expedition and had no idea what to expect. I confess, I was slightly nervous; were these people all going to be seasoned, professional hardened climbers with far more experience than myself? Would I pass muster, would they think me a worthy expedition member?

I walked into the Rox Bar, forgetting my nerves when confronted by the beautiful square bar with its gleaming array of spotless glasses.

"You must be one of us," said a voice in a thick, Texan accent.

I turned and was confronted by a very large, scary, polished-headed guy wearing a white t-shirt and khaki shorts. His thick arms and legs were covered in intricate Aztec tattoos, brightly coloured in red and black, the bold shapes contrasting with his pale skin.

The barrel-chested man grinned at me like an old friend and stuck out a hand. I shook it.

"David," he said. "But everyone calls me Lincoln."

"Lincoln, hi. I'm Jules."

His grin somehow got bigger, stretching up to the bald dome of his head. His eyes creased and almost disappeared. He guided me into the conference room.

"Come and meet everyone."

I was introduced, one by one, to the expedition team. There were climbers from a range of nationalities and professions, including Taka and Hachiro from Japan, a doctor and a bar owner, respectively; Lincoln, a property mogul, and Louise, a heart surgeon, both from the US, and Paul from New Zealand, an ex-fighter pilot who now runs a taxi business.

I was beginning to wonder whether I was going to be the only British person on the expedition when I was introduced to John – in everyday life, an actuary. We shook hands, nodding at each other with a kind of British understanding.

John would later become my room-mate when we had to share lodges and tents – we would create our own little patches of Britain on the cold slopes of the Himalayas.

I was also introduced to Donald, from the US, who was attempting to summit six 8,000-metre peaks in a year. With him were his wife, Hilary, was also trekking with us to Base Camp to support him, Elia, his photographer, and Donat and Iwan, two professional Polish climbers who had been hired to help Donald reach his goal.

The Polish climbers were scary; they had shaved heads, and were lean and wiry, without an ounce of fat between them. They looked as if they could climb Everest in their sleep.

Donald explained that he was undertaking his crazy pursuit in order to raise money for his charity – Mission 14 – which worked to put a halt to human trafficking. I was impressed with his ambition and his dedication to his cause.

The expedition doctor, Angelica, was from the Netherlands, and the chef, Bill, was another Brit. There were also four guides, three of whom were Kiwis, the other Japanese, who were hired by the expedition to offer professional support and to organise the summit attempt as a whole. There would be 20 Sherpas joining us at Everest Base Camp.

There was an excited buzz in the room; a group of people with a common purpose coming together for the first time. These were the people I was going to live with for the next two months. These were the people with whom I was going to reach the top of the world.

Just to live with people you don't know, in close quarters, for two months is hard enough...but to add Everest into the equation? Jeepers... Had I made a terrible mistake?

I offered around the chocolates Vicky had given me at the airport – that seemed a millions years ago already – as a small token of friendship with the team.

Anyone embarking on an endeavour like this will inevitably be very driven, determined, goal-oriented, successful in their daily lives and looking for a new challenge.

Success is pretty much a prerequisite, because of the sheer cost of such an expedition. So, we had a group of 'A-type' personalities, all congregating in the same space, with the same goal. This in itself can cause problems – too many chiefs!

Our team guides went through what we were going to do for the next few days. We would be heading up the Khumbu Valley, stopping at lodges en route. They seemed very knowledgeable and experienced.

"Also," one of them said, as the lecture was drawing to a close, "each of you needs to take a bottle of this with you."

He held up a bottle of hand disinfectant.

"One of the biggest reasons people fail to reach the summit of Everest isn't the weather or the tough climb – it's their stomachs."

He paused for effect.

"The Nepalese are fairly immune to anything the mountain throws at them; you guys won't be. You need to disinfect your hands before every meal, as well as after using the...facilities."

I didn't much like the idea of getting the trots at 6,000m – 'Buddha's Revenge'.

We were also advised to take two toilet rolls from the back of the room. Once we started up the Khumbu Valley, none would be provided. In fact, we were to consider ourselves lucky if there was actually anything resembling a toilet.

Just as soon as it had begun, the meeting was over. Again, I was struck with that feeling: 'what now?'

Nobody seemed to be coordinating anything for dinner... I resigned myself to the fact that I was on my own again. I went to reception and asked where would be the best place to get a drink.

"Thamel," the receptionist replied without hesitating, "go to Thamel. That's the best place for bars."

I jumped in a taxi and headed for Thamel. Sure, I'd come for Everest, but I wasn't going to miss the opportunity to see this amazing city.

The 20-minute taxi journey was a real eye-opener – but for all the wrong reasons.

The roads were pitted with potholes, which my driver made no attempt to avoid. I was thrown up, down, over in the back of the taxi, while I gripped the seat in front for dear life.

He also made no attempt to slow as cars, taxi, motorbikes, pedestrians – even animals – crossed in front of him. He wove, zigzagged, swerved down the road, all the time accelerating.

I looked over and – quite disconcertingly – he wore no expression. He looked at the road blankly as he masterfully negotiated the myriad potential catastrophes.

I gripped harder.

The taxi was absolutely knackered – all the cars were. The paint was chipping away, the seats were worn... I suspected the brakes had seen better days. The door panels were completely gone.

Still, the taxi belted through the winding roads. He made a sharp turn and dashed down a side street, narrowly avoiding pedestrians – who seemed unfazed by the whole thing.

Every so often, he hit a pothole at full throttle. There was an almighty, spine-jolting crunch, and then we were off again.

It was a wonder I didn't get whiplash.

Without warning, the taxi slammed to a halt, skidding slightly and sending up a small dust cloud.

Calmly, the driver stopped the meter and looked expectantly at me – the closest thing to a facial expression I'd seen since getting in.

I paid him and quickly jumped out of the car, closing the door behind me. A small amount of glass fell out of the wing mirror. The car screeched off down the road, bumping and lurching through potholes all the way.

I'd been in more than my fair share of road accidents – I felt almost certain I had been heading for another just then.

I stood by the side of the road, watching the taxi swerve to avoid a cyclist before disappearing from view around a corner.

Above my head, the wires from the telegraph poles crisscrossed the road like spider's webs; they were intricate, sprawling masses of spaghetti. How any of them were maintained, and how anyone received power from them was beyond my comprehension.

The sun was beginning to set, and the twisting, winding streets of the Thamel district were coming to life.

On each side of the narrow road, three-storey buildings stood in a jumbled mess, seeming to lean on each other and out over the road drunkenly. The area had a very Nepalese charm, and was alive with voices, laughter and merriment.

A man approached, asking if I was looking for somewhere to enjoy a drink.

He took me to a bar, pointed me to the entrance. I walked in and the bar was full of half-naked women. I stopped and turned around to face the guy.

"This isn't what I wanted," I said.

"Nice girls, pretty girls," he replied with a grin.

"No, no, this is not what I want. I just want a beer."

I left, despite his protestations, and walked through the

meandering streets until I stumbled across a bar with a rooftop terrace that looked and felt respectable.

I sat on the roof, looking over a busy crossroads, watching the world go by, eating a plate of chips and ketchup while sipping on a perfectly chilled pint.

I had arrived.

Scenes from the Khumbu Valley

I woke early on the morning of 30 March, comfortable and warm in my Hyatt hotel room in Kathmandu. This was to be the last time I would enjoy the luxury of a real bed in a long time, but I didn't have too much time to appreciate just how much I was going to miss it...

It was 6am and still dark outside when I walked down to the hotel lobby to join the team.

Our expedition group had been split into two, one group leaving at 7.30am and the other at 9.30am. I was in the latter, thank goodness. I hate early mornings.

Bleary-eyed, but excited, we chatted among ourselves. We had had to manhandle our two large kit bags to the designated area outside the hotel, where they'd been weighed to check they were not over the helicopter's weight limit.

Once we'd all arrived, we piled into the shuttle bus to the domestic airport, the vehicle fully laden with our huge expedition bags.

It was a bizarre airport; essentially just a huge aircraft hanger – a large, red-brick building, about 15 metres high, with a corrugated tin roof. There were no windows, but light flooded in through the open gap between the brickwork and the roof – it looked like someone had jacked the roof up three metres all around.

Massive fans, like something from a 1920s American movie, swept laboriously through the stale air below the roof, making a weak effort to ventilate the building. It was very, very hot, and there was a horribly stuffy, sweaty, spicy smell.

We made our way through what passed for Customs, flashing our passports, and a small paper tag that served as a ticket, at uninterested staff – they nodded briefly at each passer-by. We put our bags through a makeshift metal detector.

We were in for a long wait; we'd been warned of that before arriving. There didn't seem to be any obvious system in place at all.

I rested my back against one of my expedition bags, with my feet out in front of me on the rough concrete floor, gazing out on the hustle and bustle of the manic place. I was quite content, watching staff and passengers mill about, trying to locate their flights. It was an entirely different experience to anything in the UK.

Most people were trekkers or climbers, heading out for the trekking and climbing season from March to June. Most, like myself, were now slumped against their expedition bags on the airport floor.

The building was very dirty and old. There was a cacophony of sounds; live animals in cages, people shouting, planes landing – it was chaos.

By 11am, two hours after we had arrived, there was still no update on the ETA of our helicopter flight to Lukla; nothing. We just sat, chatted among ourselves and waited.

There was no departures board, so we had no idea how long we were going to have to wait. Official-looking people scurried about, trying to organise what was going on. I didn't care. I was there for two months, so there was no rush, and I was enjoying chatting to my new expedition team mates, and finding out what drove them to want to climb Everest.

There must have been 500 people, all crammed into this small space, all waiting with no information. I could make out individual expedition groups, although we had started to merge into each other in an attempt to find somewhere to sit down. Some expeditions had their names printed on their bags – Adventure Consultants, IMG, etc.

There was a bloke in a blue uniform standing next to a set of doors on the far side of the hall. Seemingly at random, he was letting groups through to the next room. There had to be some sort of a system in place, but I couldn't figure it out.

Eventually, we were told we could move through to the other hall, and we passed through an ID checkpoint into what was supposedly the 'departure lounge'.

The 'departure lounge' had a lower roof, fewer people and some black plastic chairs in rows facing each other. I found a seat with John and Paul. The two scary-looking Polish climbers – Donat and Iwan – sat opposite.

Trying to engage them in conversation, I ended up making a stupid joke that I was sure had offended them. They sat, stony-faced, staring at me, before speaking quietly together in Polish. I worried that I had already ruined Anglo-Polish relations for the duration of the trip. (My fears turned out to unfounded, and we later became firm friends.)

After my faux pas, though, the helicopter couldn't arrive soon enough. I distracted myself by watching four men crawling like ants over a huge transporter helicopter, trying to fix its propellor.

"This is us," one of the guides said at last.

We headed out and jumped into a couple of trucks that took us around the perimeter of the airport to the helicopter area.

Two helicopters had arrived to transport our group to Lukla, from where we would start our trek up the Khumbu Valley. I grabbed my bags and climbed aboard the nearest helicopter. I was joined by Lincoln, Paul and John.

As soon as we had wedged ourselves into the back of the helicopter, it took off, lifting into the sky with no effort at all. The pilot dipped the nose and we left Kathmandu behind us, heading northwest to our destination.

The flight took little more than half an hour, covering about 140km.

The views were stunning. Rough terrain sprawled away beneath us. Dirt tracks crossed the landscape, seemingly at random – I followed a tiny dirt track that wound up a hillside, with a sheer cliff face on one side. It hugged the mountainside as it twisted up the valley. Where on earth could this track lead? What destination could possibly be worth that perilous journey?

The track came to an end at the top of a mountain, outside a building. Bloody hell, I thought – that's a house. That track is the only way to get to that house.

A Nepalese woman was outside the building, tending crops on a small patch of cultivated land. She paid no attention to the helicopter as we whipped overhead.

They were *no* roads anywhere – only dirt tracks for humans and yaks... Wow. It seemed incredible that only a few miles outside Kathmandu, there were no roads...

It was truly extraordinary, looking down from the sky on this rural life. Families would have lived there for generations, tending their crops and living closely together. They would have made the long, arduous journey down the hill on foot or with a yak, and only if they really needed to get supplies or medical help.

The simplicity of that life appealed very much to me. Everything was in their own hands; there was no one saying what they could or could not do. It was like a very long ago lost age in Britain.

I stared down at the mostly empty landscape, occasionally spotting a remote house, a twisting track or a lonely yak.

The noise of the helicopter blades was deafening. I took out my headphones and plugged them into my iPhone – I borrowed a spare set of copilot headphones to cover my ears. I relaxed with AC/DC thudding in my ears, feeling as if I was in some Vietnam movie.

Before long, we arrived at Lukla.

Lukla is a tiny village resting on a mountain plateau at the top of a steep cliff, which rises some 45 metres. There are cultivated fields immediately next to the airport runway, which is the only paved surface.

The runway jutted out towards us, sloping upwards at the end before dropping off the cliff face dramatically. Taking off from Tenzing-Hillary Airport must be a white-knuckle moment, as the plane invariably drops over the cliff edge before gaining enough airspeed and momentum to actually fly. I was glad we hadn't taken the plane.

We came in to land on a bit of rough gravel next to the runway, with a stone hut in front of us. This was the airport. This was it! We disembarked quickly, grabbing whatever bags we could and running to the rough stone wall in front of us, half-crouching all the way.

The 'airport' was named after Sir Edmund Hillary and Tenzing Norgay – Tenzing-Hillary Airport – the two men who first summited Everest in 1953. I was to discover that it wasn't the only thing in the valley named after this pair.

Once our team had gathered, we were told we had to make a five-hour trek north to Monjo. The plan was to follow the Khumbu Valley for the next ten days, arriving at Base Camp around 10 April. We were taking the Thyanboche route, which passed through the Namche Bazaar, but detouring to stop at Khumjong before heading towards Pheriche and onwards to Everest.

The trek wasn't particularly difficult – the challenge was the acclimatisation – so we had to take it at a steady pace to allow our bodies to adjust to the altitude. No matter how fit you are, you cannot rush up the Khumbu Valley. It was a great opportunity to check out the landscape and to bond with some of the people on the team.

After passing through the small village of Phakding, which is positioned next to a tight turn in the flowing Dudhkosi river, we continued across an enormous suspension bridge. The valley was littered with bridges like this one, in differing states of repair. Some were old, rickety structures, while others had been recently renovated or replaced. I wondered where the money had come from to replace them, and later learned that the new suspension bridges were a gift from the Swiss.

This new bridge looked sturdy, being constructed with strong steel wires, but it was only wide enough for us to walk in single file. It spanned a gorge approximately 50 metres deep, and was 200 metres in length, spanning the gap between Nunthala and Bupsa. It seemed to stretch for miles.

Colourful rags of material – Buddhist prayer flags – had been strung all along the sides of the bridge, giving it a festive, vibrant air, making it stand out from the rich green trees carpeting the valley below. This lower part of the Khumbu Valley was not dissimilar to the Alps, with its rocky, pine-strewn mountainsides. It smelt of pine and was very beautiful. The trek was relaxing, and I felt happy, taking all this in with my new comrades.

The bridge bounced with our weight as we crossed it, enjoying the magnificent views of the Dudhkosi valley. I thought about how much the landscape must have changed, even since Hillary's days. There would have been no suspension bridges crossing the gorges then.

His expedition would have made its way down the steep incline at Nunthala, and crossed the wide river base, before scaling the other side up to Bupsa. This endeavour would have added several days on to their trek, not to mention the effects of the changes in altitude. I was very thankful this bridge had been installed, even as it swayed in a strong gust of wind.

We'd been told that the human body is able to adjust by approximately 600 vertical metres per day without suffering from adverse side effects, so it was not just for the scenery that we were proceeding up the valley at a gentle pace.

We reached Monjo at around four in the afternoon.

Monjo was a beautiful little village, situated in deep valley. It had a quaint, simple charm, with pathways of rough cobblestones. The small, single-storey stone houses were set into the mountainside, with any exposed timber painted bright blues, reds and greens.

Close to the buildings were small terraced fields, squashed into any reasonably flat area of land. These had been made by building stone walls along the hillside, then, over hundreds of years, gradually filling up the space behind the walls with earth carried from other areas until a level surface was formed. Over generations, without any proper tools, the Nepalese had managed to make many of these terraced fields on the mountainsides, and this was how they fed themselves – on a diet consisting mainly of bok choy, onions, potatoes and any other vegetable sturdy enough to survive the altitude and changeable conditions. They carried soil in wicker baskets and cultivated these tiny terraces to produce the food they needed to survive. I found this quite amazing, seeing how these people have created their lives.

We were staying in the Monjo Guest House, which was one of the many lodges situated in the Khumbu Valley to service the needs of climbers.

It had a sign outside which read: 'ECO-FRIENDLY LODGE, FINE HOME COOKING WITH ORGANIC VEGETABLES, ATTACHED BATHROOM, SOLAR HOT SHOWERS.'

It sounded great. There I was, 2,835m above sea level, and they offered all the comforts of home!

It didn't turn out quite as I was expecting...but it suited me fine on my adventure.

The guest house was like a long, stone cattle shed, with plywood partitions between each 'room'. There were two plywood bed bases topped by slender foam mattresses in each, with just enough space to get between them.

I shared a room with John: a happy choice of room-mate because he was very organised and hygienic – just the sort of person you need in such a situation, as people can quickly get very smelly with the limited washing facilities available.

The facilities were pointed out, including the solar hot shower, which consisted of very little more than a hosepipe running through a wall.

We were told not to put any paper down the toilets because the raw human sewage was dumped directly onto the vegetable patches, to fertilise the soil.

This gave a whole new meaning to the 'FINE HOME COOKING'

sign. Essentially, we were likely to be served bok choy grown with last year's expedition's poo. Somehow, I found I was suddenly slightly less hungry.

That evening, I was chatting with another climber over a beer in the guest house. The conversation turned to the loos – a hot topic – and he regaled me with a story.

"This is my second attempt at Everest," he said. "Had to turn back on the first one."

"Why's that?"

"I was at Base Camp, settled in for a week or so, when I got a bout of the shits. One night, I woke up and my stomach was in knots. I knew I had to get to the toilet sharpish. Trouble is, up at Base Camp, you can't just unzip your tent and dash to the loo – you've got to pull on your trousers, get your hiking boots on, downing jacket and pants... It was a whole routine, only it had to be carried out in double-speed."

He grinned at me.

"Anyway, I made it out of the tent somehow, dashing like mad across the rock and ice and snow. I could see the toilet tent in the distance. I was nearly there...but then, suddenly, I couldn't control myself any longer; I filled my trousers."

A not so lovely image formed in my mind.

"I cleaned myself up, sorted everything out – these things happen more often than you'd think up there. The final straw, the point where I decided to pack it all in and head home, was the following night. I kid you not, I shat my sleeping bag. It was everywhere."

Excellent...very reassuring.

"I had to call it a day," he continued. "I couldn't keep going. No matter how much I tried, I couldn't get the smell of shit out of my tent. I couldn't cope with that; it was driving me mad. I was there around four weeks, at Base Camp, staring up at Everest, waiting for my turn, but I didn't even get to set foot on her."

His face had lost some of its devillish humour.

"I knew I'd be back – I knew there would always be something missing in my life if I didn't make another attempt... so here I am!"

His face lit up in a grin again. He finished the dregs of his beer, stood and patted me on the back.

"I shouldn't worry about it too much. Everyone gets a bout. You've just got to hope it's not too bad; there's not a lot you can do."

He smiled again and left.

A member of staff dumped a large serving of homemade human poo-fertilised bok choy and potatoes onto the central table! What's a man to do? I wasn't going to climb Everest on an empty stomach, so I went and helped myself.

I tucked in...yum.

Later, after a couple more beers, I made my way back to my room to get some sleep. The mess room was the only room with electricity, so I used my head torch to navigate the gloomy stillness.

I got out my expedition sleeping bag, which was perfectly suited for cold environments, said goodnight to John, and tried to get some sleep.

In the cold, I could see my breath rising up to the ceiling. My mind was racing, filled with the excitement of the days to come. Each day was a step closer to Base Camp, a step closer to the summit of Everest.

* * * * *

The next part of our trek was to the Namche Bazaar. It was an exciting day, as we were due to catch our first glimpse of Everest in the flesh. I bolted down some breakfast – toast and boiled eggs with black tea – and headed back to my room to pack my kit into my expedition bag. I also got some water and sweets for my rucksack.

We each had a rucksack and two expedition bags. One expedition bag was being transported with us by yak. This one held our basic kit, sleeping bag, clothes, washing equipment etc. The other expedition bag, with all our climbing equipment, had gone straight up to Base Camp on the back of a yak. During the trek, we would pass hundreds of these large beasts, burdened by huge numbers of expedition bags, being egged on by Sherpas.

The yaks could be quite dangerous if you met them on a narrow path overlooking a steep drop. It was vital to ensure you were between them and the mountain. Otherwise, they were likely to push you over the edge. They went in a straight line; that was all they knew. They certainly wouldn't wait to let you pass. And it was inadvisable to get downwind of them, because they pee and fart anywhere and everywhere.

At about 11am, I came to a clearing and looked up...and there she was.

Focusing on the task in hand and avoiding the yaks, I'd nearly forgotten about her.

Everest stood, proud and remote, head and shoulders above the rest of the skyline, even at this distance. The sun glistened off her snow-capped peak and wind blew off a snowy mist, like smoke. It looked so serene, so peaceful, and yet so icy cold up there... I thought how deadly she could be.

A constant jet stream runs over the top of the mountain, so the winds can reach up to 300 kilometres per hour. From here, it all looked still, except for the plume of snowy smoke, but I knew that was likely to be an illusion. Predicting the weather is one of the main challenges involved in climbing Everest, because it is only possible to summit on a day when the jet stream will not blow you off the mountaintop. So we were very dependent on our expedition leader's ability to predict this accurately up to a week in advance. If he got it wrong, the summit push would be over.

One of our Sherpa guides walked past me and saw me appreciating the spectacle. He pointed up.

"Chomolungma," he said.

Chomolungma is the Tibetan name for Everest, which straddles the border between Nepal and Tibet. It means 'goddess of the universe'.

As a race, the Sherpas have great respect for the mountain, believing it to be holy. A huge amount of superstition and ritual has developed within their society, centred on appeasing the protective deities of the mountains they worship. If they failed to carry out these rituals or respect the mountain, they believe tragedy would befall them all.

Perhaps because of this, their relationship with Westerners hoping to climb their sacred Chomolungma can be tense and difficult. The Sherpas usually sleep and eat separately from the Western climbers – they are expert mountaineers who are paid well to guide us up the mountains, but our contact with them is generally quite minimal.

In 2013, a group of a hundred Sherpas attacked three male Western climbers – Ueli Steck, Simone Moro and Jonathan Griffith – who were climbing Everest solo. The Sherpas brandished ice axes and a violent scuffle ensued, with stones and punches being thrown. The trio only managed to escape when a female climber intervened and stood between them and the Sherpas.

The details of what actually happened are murky, but it seems the Sherpas had been laying ropes between Camps 1 and 2, for the benefit of climbers, when the unaided Western group had continued past them. The Westerners claim that they didn't interfere with the Sherpas or cause them any disrespect, but the Sherpas claimed that as the Westerners climbed past and above them, they dislodged ice and snow on to them, endangering their lives.

The confrontation ensued at Camp 2, later in the day.

It was an ugly scene – a near disaster – though fortunately nobody was hurt. But it showed just how tenuous the relationships between the Westerners and the Sherpas could be at times.

"Chomolungma," I said back to the Sherpa.

A smile broke out across his weathered face. He continued on ahead of me.

The Sherpas in our expedition, however, were a lovely bunch. They didn't speak much English, but they were professional and clearly knew their trade well. I trusted them.

Everest has had a death-rate of one in every 60 or so climbers throughout its long history, so the Sherpas were vital to the safety of our expedition.

I tore my eyes from the summit of the mountain and continued on towards Namche Bazaar.

We arrived at around three o'clock, checking into our lodge and dumping our gear.

Namche was a fascinating place, the last real stop where it was possible to get supplies before Base Camp.

The village was built into the mountain, with consecutive semi-circular terraces rising up the valley side. Buildings with brightly coloured roofs were crammed on to these terraces, creating an intricate and complicated path system – it was very easy to get lost.

There were lots of shops packed into tiny little streets – some no more than a metre across – all selling camping and hiking supplies, but a lot of the stuff was knock-off – we came to refer to the goods from these shops as 'North Fake'.

I still needed a downing jacket for Base Camp, so I went in search of one – a real one. I located a seller named Sonar who sold RAB equipment. He showed me all the import tickets for the goods, and I could tell from the stitching and materials that it was the real deal. I chatted to him for nearly an hour and he invited me up to his 'hotel' lodge that evening.

I headed back to the lodge – it was finally time for a shower.

We had been informed by the lodge staff that there were hot showers, and I suspected the hot water supply might be limited, so I didn't want to leave it too late.

There was no electricity, so the shower was solar powered. A pipe jutted out of the wall, with a tap and a jubilee clip on it. A small bit of plastic shower matting was stuck on the cold floor tiles, which made my feet freeze.

I turned the tap on... Nothing happened. I looked up into the hole and suddenly a stream of cold water fell into my face. Namche was a cold place anyway, so to take your clothes off and stand under a tiny stream of water that wasn't even lukewarm was an ordeal.

I was aware that a queue was forming outside...a queue of people waiting to try this delightful experience. They wouldn't have to wait long; I wasn't planning on hanging around.

I rubbed on some body wash, shampooing as fast as I could. When I stepped into the stream of freezing water, I let out an involuntary howl.

"You OK mate?" said a voice from outside.

"Yeah, fine," I replied. "Just a bit cold."

"I thought it was hot?"

"Yeah... So did I."

I quickly rinsed and left the shower free for the next lucky traveller.

In spite of the chill factor, it did feel good to have a wash.

I headed over to Sonar's lodge, taking him up on his invitation to look at his collection of climbing gear.

The room was like a mini-museum, with hundreds of artefacts on display in wooden cabinets along one wall, protected by glass.

He pointed out a pair of very baggy old tracksuit trousers.

"Hillary expedition," he said. They certainly looked old enough.

Next he pointed out an ice axe with an incredibly long, wooden handle.

"Hillary expedition," he said again.

I had my doubts – how anyone would be able to lug that cumbersome axe all the way up there was beyond me. I smiled, nodded, taking pictures.

Sonar's enthusiasm for the history of the mountain was clearly evident.

I headed back to the lodge to eat. Spirits were high that evening. Everyone was having a good time, so we relocated to a nearby bar.

Even here, in one of the remotest parts of Nepal, there was a bar.

On the advice of our expedition doctor, Angelica, we decided to carry out an experiment into the effects of alcohol at 3,440m. Studiously, we diligently consumed increasing amounts of alcohol, and mentally logged the impact it had on our cognitive and bodily functions.

We discovered, much to everyone's amusement, that it

caused us to have a humdinger of a night.

This was our last chance, really, to have a good party in a proper bar before the serious work began.

The bar had posters and flags lining every wall. There was a mismatched array of chairs in front of a huge plasma screen TV, which showed sport. A sound system pumped out very loud rock music. It was like being in an après ski bar – fantastic, alcohol-fuelled fun.

Here we were, at some incredible altitude, drinking lots of beers and then popping a few shots, compliments of Paul, the ex-fighter pilot. We were all of us on our dream expedition, trying to conquer the highest mountain in the world, and we were all having a blast while doing it.

There's nothing in the world quite like having a good beer in a pub to help bond with people properly. That night really brought our group together as a team. We got to know each other, our stories, our reasons for putting ourselves through this gruelling expedition. It was a much-needed blow-out.

* * * * *

I woke early, the sun beating down through the curtain-less window. I sat up cautiously, fearful of upsetting my delicate body and head.

I unzipped my sleeping bag and stood up, stretching and letting out a groan.

I felt fine... I mean, I felt like I'd had a drink, sure – but I was fine, it was unbelievable.

I chalked it up to the altitude and got ready for the day ahead.

It felt like a new day, the start of the trip proper. I had felt a lot of tension in the group at the start of the trip; no one knew each other, and we were all in a completely alien environment.

After our night in the pub, a lot of the stress had gone. I felt far more settled, more relaxed in my surroundings. We'd gone from being a group of strangers to an actual expedition team.

Outside, my heavy bags were strapped to the nearest available yak, who continued munching potatoes as if nothing had happened. I then began the three and a half hour trek to the next stop, Khumjong. This is where our expedition diverted off the normal Khumbu Valley route because our Sirdar (chief Sherpa) Purba Tashi had a lodge at Khumjong and had invited us all to stay. Khumjong village also produces the largest number of climbing Sherpas for Everest. They are all brothers, cousins, or uncles of one another.

The Sherpas are a large family group who were chased over the mountains from Tibet around 350 years ago and, finding themselves in the fertile Khumbu Valley, they settled there. They are like a race within a race, because they are Nepalese but they are also all from the Sherpas tribe/race/family.

It was a lovely day, the sun was shining, and everybody was in a positive mood. I chatted to others in the group as we steadily made our way onwards, crossing metal suspension bridges en route.

I saw Angelica, the friendly expedition doctor, up ahead, and soon caught up with her. Many of the expedition team were taking various types of drugs – Diamox, Aspirin, Paracetamol, Ibuprofen etc – in order to help them acclimatise to the altitude. It hadn't crossed my mind to do this, so I thought I'd ask Angelica's advice.

"There's loads of differing views on this," she told me. "Some people swear by it, others insist it doesn't make any difference. I'm of the latter camp – your body is naturally adjusting; it's better not to interfere. If something goes wrong, you know where you are."

"What happens then?" I said.

"We can do a few things if you're suffering from altitude problems such as HAPE. I've got lots of Viagra with me."

I looked at her.

"Sorry?"

"Viagra."

"Viagra?"

"Yes, Viagra. It relaxes the blood vessels, which is how it helps give you an erection, as blood flows more freely through the vessels. This also means blood flow can be increased at higher altitudes, reducing the risk and severity of some of the disorders associated with changes in elevation."

"Viagra?"

"Yes, Viagra," Angelica repeated. "Actually, last year, one of the guys – at least, I'm assuming it was a guy – nicked all the Viagra from my kit bag; took it all home with him. I haven't got quite as big a stash this year, because of that...so don't get any ideas."

We chatted for a while longer about health problems faced

by climbers, about high-altitude headaches, pulmonary and cerebral edemas. Once I was suitably concerned, she looked up at me and smiled.

"I wouldn't be too worried – I have plenty of Viagra," she said.

"Thank goodness for that."

We arrived at Khumjong at around four o'clock. The village was situated in an extremely remote area of Nepal, with no roads, no hospital, no sewage or mains water, and access by foot only. But there was a school, a reasonably solid structure, where we were welcomed.

There was a small ceremony in front of the school in which we were all given silk scarves – a traditional gift in this part of the world. They gave us tea and biscuits and welcomed us to their village – it was very touching.

We were told that the school was actually built in 1961 and was founded by Sir Edmund Hillary himself. The original school was a tin shed made in New Zealand, where Edmund Hillary came from, and flown to KhumJong. The shed only had two rooms, and it is still going strong today, some 50 years later, but many new buildings have been added, through kind donations, to support children who now come from the outlying villages to be educated here.

The school is run entirely by voluntary donations – the government doesn't pay for it. These children's education depends solely on the support of Westerners. Some of the children trek for miles, boarding in the school for the week, and then trekking home at the weekends. It is an arduous journey for them to take each week, in order to receive a proper education.

It was a touching experience, and we all gave as generously as we could before heading to Phurba Tashi's lodge to dump our bags. Tashi is something of a celebrity in the climbing world. He holds the world record for the total number of ascents of mountains over 8,000m, reaching these peaks a staggering 30 times during his career. This includes 21 summits of Everest.

There are many great stories about him. Supposedly, after Mark Inglis had successfully become the first double-amputee to summit Everest, Phurba Tashi carried him on his back down from the summit to Camp 4. Most people struggle to carry themselves above Camp 4, but to carry another human being? The endurance required to do that, just to make sure that this man made it back down the mountain, is unimaginable.

On another occasion he'd been employed to help a climber named David Tait in his attempt to become the first person to 'double traverse' Everest. The plan was to climb up from the Nepalese side, and then down the Tibetan side, before carrying out the reverse trip after a few days' rest.

Tait and Purba Tashi traversed Everest from Nepal to Tibet, but Tait called the expedition off after they had reached their Tibetan base, because none of the ropes had been laid on that side.

Phurba Tashi's legend had preceded him, and I was honoured to be able to stay in his lodge in Khumjong.

I'd heard rumours that there was a yeti skull on display in

Khumjong. I thought this was probably an attempt at a tourist attraction, but having trekked all this way, I just had to find out if there was any truth in the story.

I meandered through the village, weaving along wobbly paths that wound around the white stone cottages and barns. It felt very remote, with no real roads or tracks. The paths were only just wide enough for one person to walk along.

The supposed yeti skull was kept at the Tengboche Monastery, which stood on a ridge of land, with a panoramic view of the village and the Imja River below. It was an old-looking building, not spectacular but striking, standing tall against the structures surrounding it. It was the only building painted a faded, dusty red.

The monastery was surrounded by ancient-looking *mani* stones, which are flat stones inscribed with the Sanskrit legend '*Om mani padme hum*'. I'd seen this mantra before, adorning prayer wheels throughout Kathmandu – it is believed that spinning these wheels has the same effect as chanting the mantra over and over.

The phrase has no literal English translation, as the meaning of it lies beyond the construct of the words, but the central part roughly translates as 'jewel in the lotus'.

Prayer flags, similar to the ones adorning the countless suspension bridges I had crossed to get this far, flew from the tops of the higher stone collections, flapping in the wind. Their bright colours denoted the traditional elements of the Buddhist religion – earth, wind, fire, water and consciousness.

I approached the monastery and spun the prayer wheels

outside it – I wasn't sure that they'd bring me good luck, but there was no harm in shortening the odds.

I walked through the entrance gate, an old, intricate square structure with a pagoda-style top, and intertwining patterns in gold, red and green tessellated across the facade. Two ornate golden lions sat one on either side of the gate, baring their sharp teeth at those wishing to pass through.

I crossed the worn paving of the courtyard and sat on one of the many benches. Nobody else was there – it was just me and the silence.

In front of me was the *Dokhang* – the main prayer hall.

Above the doorway, five large, rectangular windows overlooked the courtyard, with ornate Nepalese decorations surrounding them. The entrance was between two thin pillars that had once been colourfully adorned, but which now looked faded. Oddly, there was a collapsible metal gate at the doorway that marked the divide, which seemed very out of place in the antique building. It was pulled open, so I was able to get inside.

A man appeared on the balcony above me, dressed in deep red monk's robes. He was old and moved very slowly towards me.

I stood up and walked over to him, putting my hands together and bowing as I drew near. He bowed back.

"Do you have the skull of the yeti here?" I asked.

He approached the edge of the balcony and shuffled down the stairs. Without a word, he walked over to the prayer hall door and turned, beckoning me with a wrinkled hand.

I felt a pulse of excitement – was he going to show me the skull? Did it actually exist?

I followed him into the prayer hall; a riot of colours covered the walls and roof. I removed my boots and walked slowly across the creaking, well-polished floorboards.

The old man put out his hand, pointing to his palm. I was prepared for this – I had been warned in advance that it was necessary to 'cross the monk's palm with silver' to get a glimpse at the skull, so I handed him $5. Still, I was amazed that even here, at this remote Buddhist monastery, 3,867m above sea level, a business opportunity is never missed.

The monk bowed and led me to a metal cabinet in the corner of the room. He felt in his pocket and took out a key, with which he opened the cabinet.

Inside was a wooden box, with glass on each side. A hefty padlock hung from the side – there was certainly a lot of security for this skull.

I peered closer, looking through the scratched glass.

There it was, in all its glory; the yeti skull of Tengboche...

The domed skull was covered in thin, dark hairs, jutting out at awkward angles. The strange item looked as if it could be part of the skull of a strange monkey, or half a coconut. It was fascinating to see – I had read that experts from around the world had visited this monastery to study this scientific curiosity, but nobody was quite sure what it belonged to... So, hey, perhaps it was the yeti – aka the "Abominable Snowman"!

It was definitely worth seeing, after a four-day trek up the Khumbu Valley.

I took a selfie with it as evidence that I'd been there, and that I'd actually managed to see it.

The story of the skull was an interesting one. I was told that the local villages used to have a combined religious festival. As the festival got bigger and bigger, the people from Khumjong decided that they wanted to run their own festival.

It was customary, when a village left, to give it a gift – normally something quite valuable or useful.

The villagers from Khumjong were given this skull – the yeti skull – a useless object that they didn't see as having any real value.

They were so disgusted by their gift that they used the skull like a football and kicked it all the way back to their village.

Now, of course, it's absolutely priceless and of extreme scientific interest. It's also great for Khumjong's tourist industry – people come to Khumjong just to see the yeti skull. They had actually been given something immensely valuable, but had thought it to be useless and worthless at the time.

At least they had the last laugh, I thought, as I thanked the monk, bowed my head and left.

I poked around the monastery for a while longer before heading back to the lodge for the evening, ahead of the dusk. It would be impossible to get back in the dark as there were no streetlights – in fact there was no electricity and there were no streets. Just winding dirt tracks between the houses and fields, which were surrounded by dry stone walls.

The lodge was one of the nicer ones we stayed at on our way up the Khumbu Valley, but mains water? Forget it. Mains sewage? Forget it. The only electricity came from solar power, and was just enough to light a bulb in the main dining area.

If you wanted to charge your phone, you had to take it to the front desk and pay $3.50 – they'd plug the phone in behind the desk and you'd come and collect it later on. If you wanted to log in to their intermittent wifi, you had to pay $5 a day. They didn't give you the wifi code either, in case you told everybody else – they took your phone from you and typed it in. It was all quite crafty, quite industrious. They were certainly embracing Western commercialism – and why not!

Phurba Tashi's family cooked a meal for us. Some of us then played cards for a short while before heading to bed.

I was sharing a room with John again, and as I lay on the thin, uncomfortable foam mattress, wrapped up in my sleeping bag, the room lit by the bright moon, I thought about the trip.

I'd been away from home for a week now and there was still a long road ahead of me. In a week's time we would be arriving at Everest Base Camp, three weeks after that we would be beginning our summit attempt.

I lay awake in the cold, unable to sleep.

* * * * *

The following days involved leapfrogging from small village to small village, staying in increasingly basic lodges on the way. After we left Khumjong, we trekked up to Phortse, where we stayed in Phurba Tashi's second lodge.

By now, I noticed the thinness of the air as it rattled through my lungs. We were at an altitude of 3,840m, the same elevation as Sauyr Zhotasy on the China-Kazakh border, one of the most prominent unclimbed peaks in the world.

The scenery became rockier, steeper and sparser – the treks became harder work. I took less time to appreciate our spectacular, and by now sparse surroundings, opting to stare instead at my feet and my walking poles as I progressed.

In Phortse, I went for a walk around the village, which consisted of many small stone houses, clustered together on a plateau high in the mountains. There were a number of terraced fields with neat stone walls surrounding them. Hundreds of years of labour must have gone into creating these delicate terraces, right next to the houses.

In these terraces, the villagers grew vegetables, and I stopped, watching a group of four women planting potatoes. They waved at me as I stood watching, so I waved back.

Nearby, there was a small stone hut, no more than two by three metres, with a blanket draped over the entrance. A small, elderly woman came out – I could see a simple bed inside.

How anybody could survive the freezing conditions of the winter and the floods of the monsoons in this hut was beyond me...but somehow this woman did.

She made her way into a nearby field and started working on the soil. She wore strange, twisted leather gloves.

I walked closer, realising that they weren't gloves at all. Her hands, through years of hard work, had become gnarled and distorted.

She looked at me; I smiled and pointed at my camera, which I held in my hands.

"Can I take a picture?"

She held out one of her leathery hands, with the palm open to the skies. I gave her a dollar, which she hurriedly pushed deep into her pocket before standing for the picture.

I thanked her, bowed and then wandered around the maze of little dirt tracks, trying to find my way back to the lodge. It took nearly half an hour of zigzagging backwards and forwards through the maze of paths. Frustratingly, I could see my destination in the distance, I just couldn't figure out which path led there.

When I finally returned, it was time for dinner, and then bed, ready for an early start the following morning.

Acclimatisation

Our plan was to climb to Lobuche Base Camp and camp for the night, before climbing back down again in the morning.

Lobuche is 6,200m high, over 1,000m higher than Mont Blanc, the highest peak in Europe. And this was supposedly a 'practice mountain'. We would not only be climbing to Lobuche Base Camp – after settling in at Everest Base Camp we'd be returning to Lobuche to climb to the summit.

We were spread out on the trek to Lobuche Base Camp. After a few hours, I turned a corner and could see a figure waving at me in the distance.

I shielded my eyes from the glaring sunlight.

The person waved with both arms above his head – what was he doing over there? That couldn't possibly be where we were staying, could it? It was off the beaten track, in a thick snowfield – but then I spotted the tents; tiny little pockets of colour buried in pure white snow against a backdrop of the snow-capped peak.

Fantastic – tents covered in snow for my first tent night.

I made my way over slowly, breathing deeply in the thin air.

We each had our own one-man expedition tent, which had already been set up for us. There was just enough room inside for my Therm-a-Rest, with my bags by my side.

I could feel the thinning air, sure, and I certainly felt a strain on my body, but I arrived at Lobuche Base Camp (BC) in fairly good spirits.

I was dreading the moment when the sun would set and all the warmth would dissipate within seconds.

We sat around in the mess tent at Lobuche BC, whiling away the hours until it was bedtime. Each of us could see only via our head torches.

Nobody wanted to go to bed. We were all dreading it.

Eventually, the time came and people started drifting off. The mess tent, now devoid of the body heat of the group, became colder and colder.

There was nothing else to do... I stood up and headed out.

I padded through the thick snow to my tent and unzipped it, untied my shoes and crawled into my sleeping bag fully clothed with beanie hat, and including my downing jacket. This wasn't the most brilliant of ideas, as the layers of insulation stop the sleeping bag from warming up so quickly, but I couldn't bear the idea of taking my clothes off in these conditions.

It was truly miserable. I could see my breath rising from my mouth in great long plumes of warm air – losing all that heat from my body. I wished I could bottle it up and shove it down into the sleeping bag to keep me warm.

I turned off the head torch and lay there in the darkness. It felt spooky and very claustrophobic, but there was nothing for it but to get on with it. It wasn't as if I could just say that I'd had enough and nip inside to a nice, warm house. I prayed that they would not find a frozen corpse in the morning.

I stayed awake for three hours, until fatigue finally got the better of me.

* * * * *

I felt even more miserable the following morning.

I awoke to the sound of somebody banging on the canvas of my tent.

"Hot tea, hot tea, hot tea!"

I sat up, shuffled forwards and unzipped the tent. A Sherpa thrust a cup of tea towards me.

"Namaste," I said.

"Namaste – hot tea."

The tea was hot and sugary; just what I needed. It tasted great in these cold conditions.

I heard the crash of a gong, which signalled breakfast – I had survived my first tent night.

It had snowed again during the night, hiding our footprints and half-burying the tents. It was almost as if we'd never been there.

Our expedition chef, Bill (the highest chef in the world), hadn't joined us on our trek up to Lobuche Base Camp; he'd gone straight to Everest BC to get the kitchen ready, so the Sherpas were cooking for us.

Bacon.

I pulled my shoes on and rushed over to the mess tent, where they were serving not only bacon, but eggs as well. This immediately cheered me up – thousands of metres above sea level and it's bacon and eggs for breakfast.

I tucked in, as if I hadn't eaten for days and I'd never tasted anything so good.

I sat back contentedly; ready to take on the day. Our plan was to hike up towards rock camp, stop for the night and then head back down and then straight on to Everest Base Camp. Tomorrow was the big day – the day we were due to arrive at Everest Base Camp.

We all set off up Lobuche, heading for the rock camp. I was the last to leave, as usual, but I made good progress. This was the first bit of real climbing that required our crampons, and there was one difficult section where we needed our harnesses and had to put in a fixed rope to scale it.

We arrived at the rock camp, where the two-man tents were already set up. I was sharing with John. It was a cold, uneventful night, and next morning John and I boiled snow on our little gas burner to make tea.

I packed up my belongings in the tent. I found myself glancing over at Everest more and more. She stood, impressively dwarfing Lobuche, tall and proud. The Goddess of the Universe.

First things first, however – it was time to visit the loo.

There were no toilet facilities at Lobuche rock camp, so we had to use plastic bags. It was illegal to shit on the mountainside, so everybody trekking down would be carrying little plastic bags filled with their own faeces.

There wasn't anywhere to get any privacy, either; I noticed a small dip in the snow... as good a place as any.

With my crampons on, I climbed down into the hole, plastic bag at the ready. There was an odd squelching sound, different from the usual crunch of the snow.

I looked down... I had trodden in somebody else's shit. Somebody had decided to use this hole, with no intention of picking up his or her waste, and there I was, standing in it.

I scraped my boot in the snow, getting rid of as much as I could, grumbling to myself all the while.

* * * * *

The following day, after trekking down Lobuche, we started on our journey to Everest Base Camp.

The route became increasingly steep, the paths more rugged and dangerous. Yaks pushed past us, urged on by Sherpas, who guided them by chucking stones at them. It was a long slog, but I was excited to get there at last.

There was one final village to pass through on our way to Base Camp – Gorak Shep, the last stop for supplies for the mountain.

The village is not inhabited all year round and exists purely to serve those going to Everest. Not even the local Nepalese wanted to stay all year round – nothing grows at this altitude – it was just rocks and ice and dirt... oh, and yak poo.

Gorak Shep – or Gorak Shit as we dubbed it – sat on the edge of a frozen lake bed, covered in sand, which would have resembled a desert, had it not been for the freezing temperatures.

The few crude structures in the village looked ready to collapse at any moment, but still, even here, there was wifi.

I sent a message to my girls, to let them know I was doing well and that we were nearly at Base Camp. I paid through the teeth for the privilege.

We didn't stay at Gorak Shit long and were warned not to eat anything before we carried on.

We were walking through the bleak, barren landscape – a world apart from the luscious, picturesque scenery further down the valley – chatting casually among ourselves. Everest Base Camp was drawing closer with each step, when suddenly we stepped into what appeared to be a graveyard.

It was a bit of a shock.

We had become used to the plaques and memorials that we had seen at periodic intervals en route to Base Camp; markers for those who had lost their lives on Everest.

But here were a whole load of them, all together. The wind whistled over the barren, treeless landscape. It was haunting, spooky.

We took a small breather and I went to look a bit closer. There were loads of small piles of rocks, with dedication plaques adorning them.

They all bore similar obituaries... 'Dedicated to so and so, born this date, died this date – loved climbing'.

It really hit home the risk people were taking – the risk I was taking – just to get to the top of this mountain. This wasn't a jolly or a walk in the park; people die regularly on Everest.

Of course, these bodies would all still be up there, preserved by the ice-cold conditions. The families have no hope of getting them down, so they have to make do with a plaque on some stones nearby. There were some really heart-rending descriptions of the dead, and small areas had sprung up with many dedication plaques to dead climbers from the same countries. There was a big Polish area, a Nepalese area, an Indian area and a Chinese area.

I walked past a large pile of rocks displaying the memorial plaques of three Indian climbers. I stopped and read each of their names.

This graveyard covered only a small amount of the total number of people Everest had claimed. Over 200 have made this mountain their final resting place; over 200 lost souls in this harshest of environments.

The colourful Buddhist prayer flags that surrounded the graveyard flapped in the wind.

I walked over to a large, marble memorial.

IN MEMORY OF GEORGE LEIGH-MALLORY & ANDREW IRVINE

LAST SEEN 8TH JUNE 1924

AND ALL THOSE WHO DIED DURING THE PIONEER EVEREST EXPEDITION.

It was odd, I thought – you never hear much about these guys. The guys who tried and failed and died. Their memories are only kept alive by these plaques in remote places, forever looking up at the mountain on which they died.

It could have been so different. It could have been Edmund

Hillary's name on this plaque, his body freezing to death on the mountainside, with George Leigh-Mallory as the decorated and celebrated hero of Everest...but it seems history only remembers the victorious, the successful.

Mallory and Irvine attempted to climb Everest in 1924, but Mallory's body was found only in 1999, when an expedition set out to discover the fate of the exploratory pair. Irvine's body has never been found. The debate about whether they actually reached the summit before meeting their fate still rages on. Mallory had a camera on him on his fateful climb and when his body was found they hoped to develop the film and find out if he had made the summit, but it was not possible, so there is no official confirmation that he reached the summit, which means the names of Mallory and Irvine are lost in the thick mist of history.

I found myself praying that my name wouldn't end up on a plaque in this eerie graveyard.

After ten minutes or so, we moved on. The mood was decidedly less buzzing, but that soon changed.

We rounded a corner and there, far across the flat valley floor, at the foot of the Khumbu Icefall, we could finally see it: Everest Base Camp (EBC).

A sea of tents spread out over approximately a kilometre, an array of yellows, blues and oranges marking the closest thing to civilisation in this desolate landscape.

As we approached, the enormity of Everest towering above it became rather intimidating. The mountain had looked massive from the moment I had first set eyes on it, but from this close proximity it filled the sky like a behemoth, dwarfing the landscape around it. Next to this undisputed queen of the skyline, even Pumori, Everest's 7,000m-high neighbour, paled into insignificance.

I could understand the religious fervour that surrounded her – I could see why she was considered holy.

We kept walking until we reached the large boulder that marked the boundary of the rudimentary settlement. 'EVEREST BASE CAMP' had been crudely etched into it and prayer flags were tied to the top, pulling outwards as if it were a maypole.

Everest Base Camp is actually on the glacier that fills and winds its way down the middle of the valley, a slow-moving ice floe covered in large rocks and boulders. It was quite easy to forget that – it certainly looked like solid land – but Base Camp was constantly on the move.

We were led by our expedition guides to the area of Base Camp that was to become our home for the next six weeks, as we acclimatised to the conditions, practised climbing and waited for our turn to attempt the peak.

A large white pod, a structure made from strong metal poles with a thick white lining pulled over the top, was to act as our social space and team briefing area.

A scattering of rugs lined the floor, with chairs and tables also dotted around. It was kind of an arctic common room, with an old gas heater for warmth. We were told this would only be turned on after five o'clock, to save fuel. When we first arrived it wasn't working at all, although it did provide heat sporadically thereafter.

There was also a television.

"This runs on one of the two solar power units," said one of the guides, "so there's only a limited amount of power. Once it's gone, it's gone – no more TV until it's able to charge the next day."

Still, I was more than happy with this arrangement – at least there was somewhere for us to spend time that wasn't our tiny, one-man tents, which we now had to kit out.

My tent looked more like a coffin, with just enough room for me to lie flat. The two-man tents up on Lobuche had been bad enough – I was dreading having to stay in this for the next six weeks.

But still, I was proud to be here. I had made it as far as Everest Base Camp.

Base Camp basics

"What on earth are you doing, Jules?" asked an American voice from behind me.

I looked over my shoulder, and saw Hilary, Donald's wife.

"Making a patio."

I was panting like a dog, absolutely cream-crackered, as I lugged over all the relatively flat stones I could find in the vicinity of my tent. With my pickaxe in hand, I knocked them into shape and fitted them into the entrance area around my tent.

It was exhausting work. Every movement took all my energy – I felt like an old man of 95. The rocks seemed to weigh double, triple what they would at home.

"A patio?"

"Yeah – I'm fed up having to put my boots on in the snow. We need some civilisation around here."

Hilary laughed – it was good to hear her laugh; she'd been suffering quite badly from altitude sickness.

"You'll have to do ours next!"

"That's what you've got your husband for," I replied, as I dropped a particularly heavy stone in place. I stopped for a breather.

Donald looked over from his seat outside the tent he shared with his wife.

"Thanks for that," he laughed. "I won't hear the end of it now."

"Sure you will – right after you've built us our patio!" said Hilary.

I laughed, before heading off in search of another rock for my entrance area.

We'd been at Base Camp for a few days now, trying to get used to the alien way of life and the very, very thin air. We ate our meals together in the mess tent, watched films in the white pod and slept alone as best we could in our bright yellow canvas coffins, except for Donald and Hilary who had a slightly larger husband-and-wife tent by pre-order. I wished I could have had one of those for myself.

In the warm sunlight of the morning, my sleeping bag was draped across the top of my tent, in an effort to dry it out. Any condensation quickly froze during the nights, creating ice crystals on the roof of the tent, waiting patiently and malevolently to shower down on you when you least expected it, making your sleeping bag wet.

A small stream trickled past the outside of my tent, cutting a meandering path through the ice.

My tent was pitched near an undulating hill in the glacier beneath us. The hill was covered in rock that had fallen into the valley, and which the glacier was carrying along as it inched its way down the valley.

I walked up the hill, panting like mad, and found a suitable rock to finish my patio, so I chipped away at it with the pickaxe until it came loose. With an effort I lifted it and slowly wobbled back to my tent and slotted it in place.

I stood up, wheezing, admiring my handiwork.

It was about time for breakfast, so I readjusted the guy lines before heading off. It was necessary to do this every couple of days, as the infinitely minute movement of the glacier caused them to slacken over time.

Breakfast was served in one of the mess tents in the centre of our camp – every day we had sausage or bacon and eggs; it was the best meal of the day.

I thanked Bill – the highest chef in the world – and took a seat at the table. Sitting in our thick, padded downing jackets, we all looked like a group of colourful Michelin Men.

Life at Base Camp had normalised relatively quickly. We'd all settled in and were excitedly counting down the days until our turn to attempt the summit. I was also counting the days until I would see Steph and Lizzie again. I missed them terribly.

We had a strict calendar of events to follow over the next few weeks, including practice climbs and hikes – we even had to camp at altitude on the 6,200m summit of Lobuche, in order to help us prepare and acclimatise for Everest.

For now, however, we ate and chatted, getting to know each other better in the relative safety of our mess tent at EBC. Unbeknown to all of us, that same mess tent would soon be serving as a hospital tent for dozens of critically injured people, its roughly carpeted floor stained with blood, the air filled with the stench of urine, treacly thick blood and death.

I finished my breakfast and headed out into the sunshine. One of the paradoxes of the mountain was that it could feel warm in the daytime, due to the sun's rays at altitude, but as soon as 4pm arrived the temperature would plummet to -15°C, and everybody would rush to their tents to get thick downing jackets and trousers on.

I sat down in the centre of the camp on a plastic storage bin and grabbed the camp guitar. I had no idea who had thought to lug the thing up there, but I was glad they had – it was a great way to pass the time...although cold fingers made it difficult to play.

The guitar was, unsurprisingly, pretty battered, and in dire need of replacement strings. I tuned her up and struck a chord. The clear twang of the strings echoed and reverberated in the valley.

It was a beautiful, alien sound in this landscape, but it felt so natural.

I pulled a C chord and sang a few lines.

I drew a sharp, rugged breath – the thin air made it very difficult.

There was clapping behind me. Hilary was standing outside her tent, pale-faced but smiling.

"Yeah, Jules," she said. "That's great!"

"My fingers are a little cold."

She came over and sat down with me.

"How are you feeling?" I asked, gently striking another chord.

"I'm struggling."

I felt very sorry for Hilary. She was only here to support her husband, Donald. She wasn't even going to attempt any climbs; Base Camp was her Everest and she'd already achieved it, but she was suffering from altitude sickness.

"They've got me on Diamox and a whole heap of other pills," she said. "I should be OK..."

She didn't look particularly convinced by her assertion.

I thought back to the lecture we all had before leaving Pheriche. We had visited the medical centre there, which had been set up by Western climbers and doctors and dealt with people suffering from altitude sickness. All on a voluntary basis, of course – the Nepalese government had higher priorities for our permit money.

The talk had been given by one of the Western doctors who had been stationed there for six months, and it was fascinating...if a little terrifying. He talked us through all the potential medical conditions associated with high-altitude, including the symptoms and prognosis.

People suffering from acute mountain sickness (AMS) were normally OK, provided they got back down to a lower altitude very quickly and took a concoction of steroid-based drugs. There were three stages of AMS that we were constantly on the lookout for. They appeared in the following order:

HAH (high-altitude headache) – a bit like being hungover, with a very bad headache.

HACE (high-altitude cerebral edema), where the brain swells with fluid and the sufferer seems drunk and disoriented.

HAPE (high-altitude pulmonary edema) – where fluid

develops in the lungs and results in a nasty cough. This could be deadly.

HAPE was especially scary. If not treated, it could result in the sufferer drowning in the fluid build-up in the lungs. Imagine that: drowning at 5,400m above sea level. The treatment was Sildenafil; its street name is "Viagra"...so there you'd be, drowning on a mountainside with a hard-on!

I felt sure Hilary was on the lower-end of the altitude sickness spectrum, but it must still have been difficult to endure. It was like being constantly slightly drunk, with no way to prevent it – your body feels distant and numb; everything spins slightly.

On top of that, you're never sure whether fluid is going to build up in your brain or in your lungs... It must be quite frightening.

"I'm sorry to hear that – I hope you feel better soon," I said. "Any requests?"

"Do you know anything by The Beatles?"

Instinctively, if a little stiffly, I pulled a G-chord on the weathered neck of the guitar, took a deep, wheezing breath, pulling as much oxygen out of the thin air as I could:

"It's been a hard day's night
And I've been working like a dog..."

It was difficult to play in such conditions, but the quality didn't really matter. It was just great to be there, sitting at Base Camp in the sunshine, playing and singing. It all felt very natural – I felt at one with my beautiful, desolate surroundings.

I played the guitar for a while, chatting with Hilary and others in the group who joined us. There was a pleasant, convivial atmosphere – everybody was pleased to be at Base Camp and we were having a good time.

The next day, we were due to climb Lobuche, as practice for Everest. We were going to spend the night in the freezing conditions at the summit, in order to prepare us for the challenges ahead at Camps 1, 2, 3 and 4 on Everest. Everest includes Base camp (at 5,400m) then Camps 1, 2, 3 and 4, and then the summit (at 8,800m).

I was looking forward to it. After all, I'd come here to climb – but I was also enjoying the downtime at Base Camp. It was nice to grab a guitar, have a chat and soak in the atmosphere of the place.

While I had some time, I decided to try to send an update to Freecom for my blog, as well as a couple of emails to Steph and Lizzie.

A Kathmandu-based company called Everest Link had set up a wifi station with two satellite dishes. They were charging $50 for 1GB of upload data, which was extortionate, but we were the epitome of a trapped market, so they could charge us pretty much whatever they wanted.

It was a very slow process, and as everybody got up in the morning, the bandwidth very quickly became full, making it impossible by midday to send any emails.

I sat down on a nearby storage bin.

First things first. I emailed a note to Steph and Lizzie. I pressed send. And waited...

I tried pressing send again, with the same result.

This continued for around ten minutes, before the email

eventually went. I stared fixedly at the green bar inching across the top of the screen. The signal was dismal.

The blog update took forever to send. I tried at first to send some pictures as well, but...no chance – the system was being hammered by the number of users. It was impossible to hold the link long enough to send anything.

The only other option was to hike down to Gorak Shit. They had a telephone mast there, a big steel mast – a repeater station. It was actually possible to get 3G signals down there... Once I had used up the remaining 800MB of data on my card, I decided to hike down there instead.

It is amazing how the lack of ability to communicate with loved ones – which we now take for granted with mobiles in the Western world – brings you down very quickly. Suddenly, as I pressed send for the umpteenth time, I started to wonder what I was even doing here? If I'm spending so much effort and money trying to communicate with the people back home, why was I here?

Sure, it was a big adventure – if a little surreal – sitting in the snow and playing guitar, but why was I really here? Could I really do another six weeks of this, and summit Everest? Freezing in my coffin every night, struggling to breathe, fighting to communicate with my loved ones... At that moment it all seemed a bit pointless.

That's the way it grabs you – one minute you are happy, the next desperately missing your loved ones and feeling down. I looked around Base Camp at the people milling about, sitting around drinking tea. Why were any of these people here?

I whiled away the rest of the day, sitting in the white pod reading the Paul McCartney autobiography I had lugged up to Base Camp with me.

A lot of the time that we weren't on practice climbs or hikes we spent in the white pod, wishing the hours of the day away. Thinking forward to summit day and going home to my daughters helped me to stay sane.

It was impossible to move quickly or to do very much at Base Camp, as the air was so thin that it was exhausting. Lying around and reading was so not me, but it was an easy option, and I was starting to slow down and enjoy it.

I tried not to think about my motivations, and just to get on with it. Some of the others, particularly those who had tried to reach the summit before but failed, were as keen as mustard. I wasn't really feeling such intensity at that time.

After dinner, I retired to the white pod to hang around the heater and watch some films. When the power ran out before the end, I realised we could wire the TV up to the solar power unit for the lights – and did so.

I was aware I was probably breaking some rules, but I didn't really care at that point. The escapism of the film was a perfect way to forget the frost constantly biting at my fingers, to expel all thoughts of the cold, dark, lonely coffin of a tent that I would soon be crawling into.

Finally, I turned off the television, zipped up my jacket and braced myself for the cold outside. I walked carefully over the ankle-breaking, rough, icy terrain, the spot of light from my head torch bobbing in front of me, illuminating a small patch of ground ahead, warning me of large rocks or ice ridges.

My tent came into view. I grabbed my wash bag and headed to the toilet tent to have a pee, clean my teeth and wash my face. It was bloody freezing – 15˚C – but it was important to maintain hygiene, healthy teeth and a routine.

I crawled into my tent, removing my boots and leaving them on my 'patio'. Zipping the tent behind me, I pulled off my thick downing jacket and trousers and got into my sleeping bag. I left my beanie hat on, as always. There was a downing head cover on the sleeping bag but I found this too claustrophobic.

It felt like crawling into bed in a freezer. The layers of clothing, the sleeping bag, the tent lining didn't seem to be doing anything; I may as well have been lying naked in the open.

I clenched my teeth, pulled my beanie hat further over my ears and shut my eyes. If the cold froze them shut, at least then I might be able to get some sleep.

If every night was going to be like this, I wondered how long I could keep this up.

Just take it one day at a time, I thought to myself, just one day at a time...

* * * * *

I needed to pee.

I tried to ignore it; I didn't want to move. My body heat had warmed up the sleeping bag, but that would dissipate in seconds if I opened it. Still, I really needed to pee.

I cursed my lack of foresight – the boxed wine had gone straight through me. Apparently it is relatively normal to pee a lot while one acclimatises.

There was nothing else for it. I had two bottles at the ready for this exact situation.

Fumbling for my head torch, I switched it on and pulled it over my beanie hat. I unzipped my sleeping bag, slid my legs out and got onto a cramped all fours. I found my pee bottle and started to pee into it, directly above my sleeping bag.

One false move and the sleeping bag would be soaked in smelly pee.

I finished, screwed the top on the pee bottle and slid back into my now cold sleeping bag. I was tempted to bring the pee bottle in with me, to help keep me warm, but resisted that urge – if it leaked in the night I would smell like hell the next day.

During that night, I woke regularly, my bladder screaming. Each time it was an even more complicated process, using the bottles to relieve myself. As they filled, the operation became riskier.

My eyes opened once more – only this time it was bright. The sun illuminated the yellow canvas of my coffin.

I had made it.

I unzipped my sleeping bag and immediately a wash of cold air flooded in like freezing water. I pulled on my thick downing jacket and downing trousers over my climbing trousers.

Carefully, I shimmied out, taking great care not to disturb the tent; shimmering ice crystals had formed in the night, hanging down from the canvas of the tent above me like a million skinny frozen bats, ready to drop down on to my face at the slightest touch.

I unzipped the internal entrance of my tent and sat with my feet over the porch to put on my boots. Once I was completely covered, ready for the elements, I unzipped the front of the tent.

Snow poured in.

I cursed the mini-avalanche as it poured over my feet.

It had snowed again in the night – unusual for this time of year – so I had to dig my way out of my tent. I pushed against the wall of snow, pushing it away from the entrance, and crawled out.

Base Camp was covered in a thick layer of fresh snow, two foot deep in places. The tracks and many of the large stones and rocks by which I navigated had been covered.

It looked almost entirely new, a freshly re-made Base Camp for the new day.

Today was Lobuche. We were climbing the 6,145m mountain today, and staying the night near the summit.

Shit – the fresh snow was going to make it even harder going, but I was excited to get out of the camp and get climbing.

My head ached from the cheap wine.

It was a risk, drinking the wine. Either you'd feel rough all night long and it'd make things infinitely worse, or you'd keel over in your tent and forget your worries, forget that you're at 5,400m, at -15°C, with very little oxygen.

I'd actually had quite a good night's sleep.

A Sherpa was doing the rounds, knocking on tents handing out cups of tea. He was a very welcome sight indeed.

He approached me.

"Namaste."

"Namaste."

He poured me a hot mug of sugary tea and then walked on. I thanked him from the bottom of my heart.

It wasn't all bad, I thought – at least the tea would sort out my headache, prepare me for the day ahead.

I was wrong about that.

I took a sip of the tea – it was warm and soothing as it slipped down my throat. But then…I immediately felt a discomfort in my stomach; it twisted and convulsed.

My eyes widened in panic. Hastily I put my cup down on the ground, it toppled over and spilt, staining the pure white snow a murky brown.

My mind flashed back to the guy at the lodge, about not making it to the loo…

Buddha's Revenge…

I rushed in the direction of the toilet tent as fast as I could, avoiding the littered stones and rocks in my path.

"Morning Jules," Paul shouted at me as I dashed past.

There was no time to respond – the panicked look on my pallid face was enough.

My body had suddenly become my enemy. I was locked in a battle to control the whole thing. I clenched by buttocks as I half-ran, half-waddled, to the toilet tent.

It came into view.

Almost there.

I dived inside the toilet tent, but the canvas cover to the 'sit-down' section was closed and zipped. Shit...shit, shit, shit.

There was somebody in there.

"Are you going to be long? I'm desperate," I shouted.

It was all going to come out; I could feel it. The colour had drained from my face as I clenched every available muscle in my body in an attempt to prevent the inevitable.

I heard the rustle of somebody standing – they seemed to be moving in slow motion.

"Come on, hurry up! I'm going to shit myself!"

The zip opened.

"Hallo Jules!"

Iwan grinned at me, standing in the doorway.

"I need..." I managed to say, trying to see a way past him.

Iwan laughed, stepping aside slowly.

"All yours, my friend."

I dashed in, pulled the zip closed, ripped my trousers down, sat down with a crash and...wallop. I felt my insides explode outwards.

The toilet was a wooden seat screwed crudely on top of a table, with a big sack underneath it to collect all the shit. The stench from that was already pretty unbearable, with the combined human waste of our entire expedition.

But the relief was intense.

I sat there, freezing cold, shivering as my bowels evacuated. It felt so good.

Eventually, I hobbled back to my tent. Iwan grinned and

waved at me as I passed; I stuck a finger up and he laughed.

I crawled back into my tent and removed my trousers and underpants. Luckily, my essential mountain climbing equipment included babywipes, so I was able to clean myself up.

It wasn't so glamorous, this mountain climbing business, A lot of it was about things like trying not to shit yourself after an early morning cup of tea. But these details don't make it into most accounts of mountaineering derring-do.

I cleaned myself up, put on a new pair of underpants, dressed again, and headed off to breakfast.

Climbing Lobuche in alpha mode

As we ate the sausage, toast, scrambled egg and tomatoes prepared for us by Bill, who wouldn't be joining us on our trek to Lobuche, we were given the usual morning briefing.

The guides stood at the top of the mess tent and talked us through our route. We would arrive at Lobuche Base Camp that day, before crampon work the following day, and hiking up to Rock Camp later in the week. We were due to climb to the summit on Sunday, stay two nights just below the summit, then climb down for breakfast at Lobuche BC and head back to Everest BC the same day.

To put this into perspective, the highest mountain in Europe, Mont Blanc, is only 4,809m. We would be camping nearly 50 per cent higher than the highest mountain in Europe.

We would be hiking from Base Camp back down to Gorak Shit, which would take about an hour and half. Then we'd head on to Lobuche, which was another two hours.

I was quite excited, looking forward to doing some actual climbing, to see how I stacked up against the other guys and girls. We had three girls on our expedition: Louise, the heart surgeon, Sheila, the doctor from another expedition, and Aayusha, a Nepalese woman from Khumjong. If she could summit, she would be able to earn a living as a Sherpa guide, but as not many women climb, it was difficult for her to get started, so our expedition was sponsoring her.

"One more thing," said one of the guides. "It has come to our attention that last night someone rigged the spare solar power unit to the television."

I focused on shovelling scrambled egg into my mouth.

"We know who it was." I could feel all eyes on me as I looked up serenely. The guides were staring at me as if I'd committed some sort of heinous crime. "Do not let it happen again."

It all felt very strange. Here we were, a group of adults who had paid no small amount to be on this expedition, and these guys were acting like we were a bunch of naughty school kids. It didn't sit well with me; we were equals all trying to achieve the same goal. No one person was better or more important than another.

Unfortunately, there was no democracy on Everest – the rule of our expedition leader was very rarely challenged. People generally paid their money and shut their mouths, doing as they were told so as not to rock the boat.

That simply wasn't how I rolled. I am used to being part of the decision-making process of anything I am participating in, and I found it irksome when we were treated so much as mere subordinates.

The guides ended their morning announcements and everybody began slowly filing out to collect their equipment.

Due to my difficult morning, I'd decided to relax a little after breakfast before setting off. The expedition was due to leave at ten o'clock, and I watched them go. I didn't see the need to rush; we had all day, and the trek should only take three hours.

At 10.22am, one of the guides saw me sitting having a cup of Her Maj's finest by the mess tent.

"What are you doing, still here? You should have left!"

"I'm just having a cup of Her Majesty's finest."

Bill looked over at me in disbelief. I don't think he could believe I was questioning a guide; everybody else treated them as if they were oracles of the mountain – they loved that.

"You need to get a move on!"

I finished my tea at a leisurely pace. There was no way I was going to rush; I was a quick walker, so I was pretty sure I'd catch a few of the team up along the way.

I took a sip of lukewarm tea. Two bollockings in one morning. It'd be a miracle if I made it another six weeks to summit day...

Lobuche is the perfect practice mountain for Everest – it has similar conditions, but you don't have to pass through the Khumbu Icefall to get to it, and by all accounts, you want to do that as little as possible, due to the very high risk of avalanches and collapsing seracs in the Icefall.

The trek to Lobuche was considered a stroll – a walk in the park – but it wasn't. If you imagine trekking in the Welsh mountains, it was nothing like that. The paths were slippery with ice, with great lumps of rock everywhere. There was no real path, and at points we had to scramble over rocks.

On any other day, this would have been fine for me – I would have enjoyed it. But the old guts were reeling all the way; I could feel my sphincter twitching.

I'd loaded up on babywipes and hand disinfectant. I'd come prepared for the worst. I'd also visited the doc before setting off to ask if she had any Imodium – she had kindly obliged.

I soon caught up with the others, but decided to stop off at Gorak Shit for some lunch. Louise and John joined me.

We had been told not to eat anything from Gorak Shit; that it was all a bit dodgy. But I was hungry, so I did anyway. I couldn't exactly make my stomach any worse.

I had hot noodles and vegetables, as well as lemon tea, and it tasted good. It was better than good, actually. I started to suspect the warnings we had received were another instance of the guides trying to keep us in line, and to ensure that we only bought food at places with which they had deals.

We sat at Gorak Shit for a couple of hours, drinking lemon tea and trying to send some emails. The level of wifi service was as terrible as usual. In the UK, it would have caused a riot. But you just have to make the best of it. At least it was better than Base Camp; emails did actually get sent – on the sixth, seventh or eighth attempt.

Eventually we set off again, arriving at Lobuche Base Camp at around four o'clock.

We were now slightly lower in altitude, as Lobuche Base Camp was at about 4,600m, as opposed to the 5,300m of Everest Base Camp. I could feel it as I trekked towards Lobuche BC. The air seemed to thicken, become more full. I could breathe more easily, richly.

We were issued with tents again, so I stowed my gear in mine. There was no white pod at Lobuche BC, no entertainment at all. It was a much more basic affair than Everest BC.

Over the next couple of days, we practised 'pointing' on the ice seracs – vast chunks of ice, about 30 metres long and 25 metres high. The Sherpas would attach a rope to the top of the serac. We then had to climb up this rope, using our jumars and crampons, sticking the front spikes of the crampons into the ice for grip, and hauling ourselves up using the jumar.

After this, we hiked up to Rock Camp to prepare for our final ascent. This was a relatively easy climb. It was like a very rocky Snowdon, not too steep and with only one really nasty bit where it was necessary to rope up and put on crampons to shimmy along a ledge. Rock Camp is a relatively flat plateau half way to the summit.

We came prepared for our stay at the top of the mountain, with boil-in-the-bag food and warm weather gear stuffed into our rucksacks.

At Rock Camp, there were fewer tents than at Lobuche BC – we had to double up. I was told to share with John again. Only problem was fitting into the damned thing – we are both tall – I'm six foot three, and John is over six foot.

We squeezed in, pushing our rucksacks down to one end of the tent and our boots in the other. There was nothing else to do at Rock Camp, and, as it was getting late, everybody stayed in their tents.

We had a tiny gas stove to cook food at the opening of the

tent. I lit it and grabbed two pans, one of which I filled with snow. I melted this and made us both a cup of Her Maj's finest with the tea bags and powdered milk I had brought with me. It was heaven, clutching the warm cups in our gloved hands. The heat from the stove barely warmed up the tent.

We cooked some noodle soup for a makeshift starter before our boil-in-the-bag main courses. Of course, at altitude, the water took much longer to boil, so our main courses took a long time – 30 minutes to boil the water and then another 30 to heat the pouch of grub. But hell, it wasn't like we were going anywhere anyway.

So we sat there, squashed into our small tent, hulking over a tiny gas stove as our food bubbled away on it.

I had *chilli con carne* and John had sausage and beans. It was the best *chilli con carne* I think I have ever tasted, but anything warm with a strong flavour tasted like Michelin-starred cuisine in those conditions.

Unfortunately, at altitude, the digestive system is...not as good. And with sausage and beans and *chilli con carne* came the resulting wind.

There we were, two big grown men preparing to climb the highest mountain in the world, sitting in our tent, farting like troopers, laughing. We didn't care much; we'd lost it really. We hadn't been able to wash properly for three days, so it didn't matter a jot.

I just prayed that the Imodium did its job properly.

* * * * *

The night was a particularly rough one. As I started to nod off, John, already snoring, turned over to face me. He breathed right into my face, sausage and beans breath, from far too close. I wouldn't let my girlfriend get that close if she'd eaten that.

I did my best to turn away, avoiding the cold canvas. It was bloody freezing, -10°C at least. Eventually, I nodded off.

In the night, I woke to a sound of running water. Where was that coming from?

I sat up on my elbows, looked around in the gloom.

I could still hear the sound of trickling water. Was I dreaming?

"Sorry mate," said the sleepy voice of John.

John was kneeling, arse in my face, peeing into his bottle. It could be worse, I thought... At least he'd had the decency to pee in the bottle and not on me.

Eventually, thank goodness, morning came. I opened my eyes and looked up at the roof of the tent, just as John turned over, banging the side of the tent and dislodging the ice crystals from the roof. As they rained down on me, I swore and tried to avoid them – not a good move, as this only served to dislodge more. They went on my face, in my eyes and all over my sleeping bag.

I sat up on my elbows.

"Morning John – thanks for the shower."

John groaned.

I unzipped the tent, and snow cascaded onto the floor through the unzipped opening.

"Snowing again."

John groaned.

It was six in the morning and the sun hadn't yet risen. There was a thick fog hanging in the valley below and fresh deep snow everywhere. It all looked very still, very white, very beautiful, and very cold. I watched my breath rise in a long stream from my mouth.

After I dressed – downing jacket, downing trousers, thick socks, boots – I crawled out of the tent. I could just about make out the silhouettes of the other tents – small shadows in the distance.

Today, we were off to the summit of Lobuche. I was excited.

I could see others moving around in the fog, shivering in the freezing environment, hands tucked firmly in their armpits.

One of the shadows started talking to me.

"Hi Jules," said a female voice.

"Hello?"

I was fairly certain it was Louise – she had a distinct American accent – but the wind and the cold seemed to distort the sound, so I couldn't be sure.

The shadow came closer; suddenly I could see the previously hidden face.

"Didn't recognise me?" she said, eyes bright – they were the only part of her face that was not covered. "We're leaving at seven."

"Seven? Why?"

"Orders."

"But we've got nothing else to do today. We'll just be sitting at the summit, freezing our arses off all day."

"We'd just be freezing our asses off here."

It was too cold to debate – I just conceded defeat. It's easier at -10°C. We had five hours to achieve the climb, trudging through the deep fresh snow. I didn't envy the people at the front, breaking trail through the thick snow. It was going to be very, very hard work, so I hung back. Nothing new there, then.

I had breakfast with John, perched in the end of our tent again. We melted some snow and made tea, followed by crushed Weetabix with powdered milk, sugar and boiling water, all mixed up – my porridgey morning kick-start. It tasted great.

My mouth throbbed from a cold sore that had developed during the night. Somehow, it felt a million times worse up here on the mountainside.

It was basically a mild herpes attack, which meant that I was run down. Not surprising at 5,000m, but it was the last thing I needed on Lobuche summit day. It was going to be tough enough getting to the summit anyway.

The plan was for everybody to leave around 7am. I left a little after 7.30 – John had gone on ahead. I calculated we'd be hitting the summit by midday, and then have nothing to do except hang around on the summit all afternoon, so no point in rushing.

There was a very competitive spirit within the group. So not only were we climbing to reach the summit, we were also, to a certain extent, competing against each other. You don't want to get thrown off the expedition – you don't want them to turn round and say: "You're not up to it, you're not going to get your bash at Everest" – so we were competing against each other to prove that we were good enough, to prove that we could be one of the first ones up Everest this year.

I soon caught up with the back marker and had to veer off the beaten track of freshly crushed snow to make my own trail to get past. Boy, that was hard work. I cut back on to the beaten track.

I passed another guy, and another. There was no stopping to chat on this hike; the air was too thin, and all of our focus was on keeping going.

I probably went too fast in the end, as I was trying to make up ground. I felt the air burn as it entered my lungs, my calf muscles were screaming with each step.

As we got higher, each step became slower, more laborious. I drew as deep a breath as I could and forced myself into taking the next step. Then I'd pant deeply, three breaths, and take the next step. If you don't pace yourself right, you take five steps and almost collapse. There's very little oxygen in the system, it's vital to go at a steady pace, to concentrate on getting the pace right.

We were all wearing crampons over our climbing boots, and carrying our rucksacks with all our food and equipment. It was a lot of stuff, and it wasn't light.

I was tired, particularly with the cold sore attack, In fact, I was completely shattered. This was the highest altitude I'd ever climbed at, and each step only made it higher. This was new territory, and I was nervous, but also eager to prove I could do it.

Ahead of me and behind me, I could see the silhouettes of the others through the fog, heads bent, shoulders hunched, shuffling onwards like zombies.

"We're going to take a break," said a voice over the air.

I really needed that. We were free walking at this point – none of us was attached to a rope – but there were some fixed ropes slightly higher. And then we'd have to start using the jumar to climb the top sections.

We stopped, gathered in a group in silence, panting and gulping water from our bottles. I also crunched on a ginger biscuit. I tried to remain standing as straight as I could, ignoring the screams of my muscles. 'This isn't even Everest,' I kept telling myself. 'Pull yourself together!'

After five minutes, we trudged on again – pant, pant, step, pant, pant, step – soon we came to the fixed ropes.

Each in turn, we hooked on our jumars and continued.

Pant, pant, step, push the jumar up, pant, pant, step.

It started to get steeper; each step became harder than the last. I couldn't stop; I wouldn't allow myself to stop. If I did, I would never start again.

To the right, out of nowhere, there was a sudden massive drop-off. I looked down. It seemed a around a kilometre of sheer drop. An unimaginable distance. I felt the hairs on the back of my neck prickle.

I was bloody glad I was fastened to the rope.

I was dizzy, the thinning air and the lack of oxygen made my muscles feel heavy, dead. Without that rope, I wouldn't trust myself to stay balanced; I would be halfway down that drop before I even realised what was going on.

We stopped again, on a small plateau.

"We're about halfway," somebody said.

Bloody hellfire.

There wasn't much left in the tank, I was fighting against the will of my body and half of my brain. Then that news about being only half way...

This was going to be a killer. I gulped some more water and ate some gummy bears.

We pushed on again. I focused on putting one foot in front of the other, then the other again...repeating. Left foot, right foot...the only thoughts going through my brain.

It felt as if I would never get up. It would take forever. I would be climbing this mountain forever. It wasn't even Everest.

We arrived at a slope, a very steep slope, around 50 degrees.

It was exhausting. I pulled on the rope with my jumar like mad, fighting against gravity as it tried to drag me back down. Right foot, pant, pant, pant, left foot, pant, pant, pant, right foot, pant, pant, pant, left...right...left...right...left...

I could hear Lincoln coming up behind me, and Taka just behind him. I could see Louise ahead.

I was desperate not to let Lincoln pass.

I wanted to keep my position. Crazy, really, when it doesn't matter where you come, but you get obsessed around Everest.

My mouth ached, the cold sore burned. I struggled on.

Right, pant, pant...left, pant, pant...right, pant, pant...left, pant, pant, pant. I collapsed on my hands and knees.

The deep breaths filled my lungs with nothing at all.

Lincoln caught up with me.

"Are you alright?"

I was now on all fours. "Yeah, yeah, fine...fine,' I lied. 'Crack on, you're doing great."

Lincoln carried on.

I wasn't fine. I felt like I was dying on the spot. I was absolutely exhausted.

I looked up. How bloody far was this? When was it going to end?

I couldn't see far in the fog that swirled about me. It was impossible to judge how long it was still going to take.

With every ounce of strength I had, I hoisted myself to my feet. I was desperate to keep my place on the rope, not to let anybody else pass me. I looked back. I could make out Taka in the distance behind me.

The thin, thin air rattled uselessly through my lungs. It felt as if somebody had put a plastic bag over my head and then told me to run up and down the stairs a million times. There was no air; there was just no bloody oxygen.

My rib cage felt as if it was about to explode from my long, drawn-out breaths.

I kept going... Left, pant, pant, pant...right, pant, pant, pant... left... How long? Right...left... I can't keep...

"You're nearly at the top!"

The voice floated down serenely, heavenly.

I took five more steps, collapsing again on my hands and knees, panting like a sick dog. I pulled myself up, managed five more, collapsed again. I stood up, clenched my frozen jaw... Left, pant, pant, pant...right, pant, pant, pant...left...

I looked down at my feet. There was nothing else in the world right now apart from the frozen, solid ground in front of me.

Then, as suddenly as I wasn't, I was there. I had reached the top.

I didn't want to look as if I was in a bad way in front of the guides who were already there. I didn't want to show them that I was knackered. I stood at the top of Lobuche Mountain, every fibre of my body screaming for me to lie down, but I didn't.

I walked the ten metres over to the others, dropped my rucksack to the floor and sat down with them.

"You OK?" asked one of the guides.

"Yeah, fine," I lied.

I had finished well, and I now slumped onto my rucksack... I was so tired.

But I had made it.

Lincoln, who had overtaken me in the last section, grinned his huge wide happy grin at me.

"Well done, buddy," he said.

I nodded.

"Well done to you too bud – you beat me up here; great job."

Louise and Paul were also there, getting their breath back, trying to recover.

I had come fourth, out of the group of ten. Considering I had left later than everybody else, I was quite pleased with myself. It wasn't a race; I knew that. I was just eager to prove myself worthy of being a part of the expedition team. I didn't want to seem as if I didn't know what I was doing, and I didn't want to be the slow one at the back, holding everybody else up.

In all likelihood, we were going to be split into two teams to tackle Everest, with the strongest team going first. I wanted to be in that team if I could. To be left back at Base Camp, and for the first group to return having successfully summited, would be really hard. What if the weather changed, and the second group didn't get their shot?

We had been given five hours as a rough estimate to summit Lobuche. I looked at my watch, rubbing off the frost that had accumulated on the face. It was 10.30. It had taken the four of us only three hours – not bad.

Taka arrived and sat down with us, panting. I patted him on the back and he smiled.

"Well done, mate."

Now I could breathe again, and the lactic acid was starting to drain from my muscles, I looked around the immediate area where we would be camping. We were about 100m from the actual summit of Lobuche, on a natural plateau of about seven square metres.

Five tents had been pitched for us to stay the two nights. I decided to go and investigate, to try to find one that didn't slope too severely, one that wasn't too close to the cliff edge.

I found a good tent with a view towards Everest and shoved my bag into it, claiming it for John and me.

I decided to dig a small trench in the snow inside the front section of our tent, so that we didn't have to sit with our knees around our ears while we cooked. It meant we could actually sit in the main part of the tent, with our feet in a hole in the front part of the tent and with the lining unzipped. We would at least be a little more comfortable.

John arrived half an hour later, panting and wheezing. He was the last of the 10 of us, but he was strong, too, and we'd all made it up in three and a half hours. It was very impressive; some people don't even make it in five hours, others don't make it up at all. We were a pretty unusual group, according to the guides; we were all pretty strong, and most of the expeditions have one or two stragglers, but not ours.

"What's the hole for?" John asked, between gasps of air.

"It's for our feet, so we can sit in here properly."

He smiled the smile of an exhausted man.

"We can leave a little ridge in the middle. We can put the stove on it and we can sit either side," I said.

That night, all of us spent the evening huddled in our own tents, zipped up, sitting around tiny camp stoves making dinner.

"A cup of tea before dinner, John?"

"Yes, that'd be lovely, thank you very much."

"Do you want some powdered milk with that?"

"Oh super, yes, please."

"Sugar?"

"Just a little, as we're here, for a treat."

It was a surreal experience – sitting in a tent very high up in the world, with someone I had met just over a month ago, drinking tea. We made our very own little patch of England at the summit of Lobuche. The tent was all that was between us and death, as the temperature outside plummeted to -15°C once more.

"What shall we have next? Shall we have the soup or the main course?"

"Oh, let's have a soup course."

We had noodle soup next. We had to work together as a team. With our downing suits on, we looked like two very big Michelin Men, and our thick gloves made it very difficult to open packets and handle cutlery.

After dinner, we had spotted dick and custard for dessert. Nobody but the English wanted to touch these puddings with a barge pole, so there were loads of the packets for John and me. It was great actually; everybody else was missing out. I'm not sure the Americans knew what it was, but anything with a name like 'Spotted Dick' was to be avoided at all costs!

So there we sat, with our feet shoved in the holes I'd dug in the ice, eating dinner, drinking cups of tea and chatting away quite happily for the evening.

I had a small music speaker with me, so I used my iPhone to play some songs. The Beatles came on, so we sang along loudly. Unfortunately, one of the guides didn't appreciate our musical prowess.

"Shut the fuck up!"

Heathens.

We sang louder, of course – it was very rude of them, actually; there we were doing a few Beatles numbers, serenading our little group on the summit of Lobuche, and somebody was telling me to shut the fuck up. Outrageous!

By about nine o'clock, the makeshift campsite had gone quiet. I'd turned the music off and the chatter from the other tents slowly diminished. There was very little to do, so I settled down to another night wedged into my slightly too small sleeping bag, praying that I wouldn't need to pee.

* * * * *

I woke in the morning to a shower of icicles cascading down from the canvas lining of the tent as John got up. "Bollocks," I thought. I couldn't be bothered to move. What was the point? We were staying there for another day and night *acclimatising* – so there was no point in rushing to do anything. There was nothing to do.

"Cup of tea?" John asked.

Without waiting for my answer, he sat up and fired up the stove to make a couple of cups of Her Maj's finest. That was something worth moving for.

I felt tired and cold, but I picked my head up off my inflatable pillow and sat up.

I ate crushed Weetabix, with powdered milk, lots of sugar and hot water for breakfast.

Soon, there was movement around the camp, so John and I pulled on our boots and crawled out of the tent.

Paul and Lincoln stood looking up at the summit.

"It's a shame really," Paul said.

"What's that?"

"To come all this way and not go to the very top."

I looked up at the summit of Lobuche, about 100 metres away from where we were camped, along a very, very narrow ridge.

"We could just walk up that ridge," said Lincoln.

That ridge looked horrible. It was a skinny, narrow thing with a massive drop on either side. There was no rope.

"Wouldn't it be fun to actually walk up the ridge to the summit?"

"No, that would not be fun at all," I said. "That would be stupid."

Ten minutes later, the guides walked over.

"We're doing the summit, if anyone wants to come."

Oh shit, I thought. From what I know of my expedition buddies, most of them will want to do it. It's my day off at 6,200m, and I will now be forced, through peer pressure, to climb this bloody ridge. And if I fall off, it's certain death!

We didn't have enough rope to tie ourselves together, so we did the ridge in sections, with our ice axes as anchor points for the rope. Not only were we climbing the ridge, but we had no ice axes in our hands, as they were all stuck in the snow securing the short safety rope which held us on the tiny mountain ridge.

It was sheer stupidity; the whole expedition could have been wiped out in an instant by one wrong step. There was every chance that the ice might crack and the snow would collapse, taking us all down in an almighty avalanche.

We got halfway along the ridge and ran out of rope. So we

had to stop to haul the rope in and lay it out again on the final section to Lobuche summit. It was a very tense few minutes.

I took my iPhone out, hitting play on iTunes.

I sang along with Paul McCartney's *Fool on the hill* as we stood there. It brought a smile to everybody's faces.

We were ready for the next section, so I put the phone away and inched up the treacherous ridge to the summit of the mountain.

Soon, we were huddled on the ridiculously small summit – about two square metres, with a kilometre drop on three sides.

I looked out across the landscape. The fog from the previous day had lifted, so we could see for miles. There was only one point that would have commanded a better view... We could see Everest; she seemed to mock Lobuche, towering over her, belittling the effort it had taken us to get here.

"Next stop, Everest."

We made our way back down to the plateau and settled in for another night – tea, soup, and our boil-in-the-bags, followed by more spotted dick and custard.

The following morning, we packed up our stuff and headed back down the mountain. Once again, my leisurely start earned me admonishment from the guides. Boy, this downhill thing was great! I was moving at a steady pace, arm-wrapping the rope as I descended. Arm-wrapping is a common climbing technique, used where the slope is steep but not vertical. You wrap the rope around one arm and grip with the same hand. This then creates friction, slowing your rate of descent. I was motored now.

I could see someone ahead of me – I think it was Hachiro. When we reached the rope fixing point, I nipped past him. I continued doing this, catching up and passing members of the team until I was near the front.

I could see Louise, Paul and Aayusha ahead. I had my work cut out to catch up with them; they were fast.

As we neared Rock Camp, I was right behind Louise and Paul, but Aayusha was still a way ahead. Bloody hell, was she fast!

As we came in to Rock Camp, she was squatting to pee in the snow: when you've gotta go, you've gotta go.

We stopped at Rock Camp for a quick break; I gulped down some water and a Mars Bar.

"You coming Jules?" said Louise.

Jeepers, I'd hardly caught my breath!

Ever up for a challenge, and wishing to be one of the first down – just to prove a point to the grouchy guide that morning, I pulled myself up and slung my rucksack over my shoulders.

We had overtaken Aayusha at Rock Camp – she'd stayed for slightly longer.

We moved on, clipped into the rope, and carefully manoeuvred along the narrow ledge, and then down some man-made steps. At the bottom, we had to remove our crampons – it was now a case of clambering over massive piles of rock for about half a mile, all the way back to Lobuche BC.

"You get going," said Louise. "I'll be right behind you."

So off I went, clambering over boulder after boulder. I could get my breath now – the air was thicker – but I knew I'd slightly overcooked the top section and I was absolutely knackered.

Louise would be right on my heels, and Aayusha couldn't be far behind us – she was fast. I was on the last half kilometre. I could see Lobuche BC. I looked behind me and there was no sign of Louise, but I could see Aayusha approaching fast, with one of the guides following closely.

There was no way they were going to beat me back.

I stretched out my legs and picked up the pace, thinking of the hot, steaming mug of tea waiting for me in the mess tent at Lobuche BC. I was almost exploding with the effort, but I was determined to get down first.

I was closing in…50 metres…20 metres…ten metres… five…

And I was there! I kept going, straight into the mess tent and slumped down in a chair.

Five seconds later, Aayusha came in. I was pleased to see that she, too, was exhausted. The guide arrived not long after.

"Good work, guys," he said, red-faced, before disappearing off to his tent.

I sat there, unable to move, with white froth and dried skin stuck to my lips, trying my best to look as if it was all in a day's work. How the hell I was going to manage the three-hour trek back up to Everest BC later in the day, I had no idea…

We would be remaining at Everest BC until our summit day, which would be around five weeks from now. I felt ready; I felt confident, and I felt terribly excited. We just had to hope that everything went according to plan in the next few weeks…

Avalanche aftershock

But it didn't, of course. The avalanche saw to that. A week or so later that wall of snow and ice had fallen out of the sky and buried me alive in my yellow plastic coffin..

I was burrowing my head deep into my Therm-a-Rest, as if trying to dig my way into the earth – desperate to protect my head and hold onto my six square feet of ground.

I couldn't stop thinking about the lake a few metres behind me, the same one that I had absentmindedly stared across on countless occasions over the past couple of weeks. I couldn't stop thinking it would soon become my watery grave. I was almost certain the avalanche would pick me up, wrapped in my tent like a sweet in its wrapper, and throw me unceremoniously into the freezing water.

There would be nothing I could do – I would be unable to escape the confines of the tent, and even if I did, the cold of the water would finish me off, and I'd be submerged under the icy surface.

BAM!! The whole tent rocked up, fighting against the force of the advancing snow. I felt a vast weight of snow pounding down on me. No time to zip up the tent, and behind me, ice and snow were blasting their way in. The noise was indescribable, and the tent was crammed with ice in milliseconds. It was also being lifted off the ground, straining against its guy lines.

My whole body was pressed as hard as I could push it down into the Therm-a-Rest.

Then, just as suddenly as it had begun, the main force of the avalanche had passed.

I tried to push up on to my hands and knees. The snow was heavy on my back as I pushed. Eventually, I shook free of it, and instinctively started digging out my expedition bags and electrical equipment. I quickly brushed off the snow, then hurried to the tent zip. Snow and wind were still piling and howling into the tent.

I grabbed the zip and pulled it hard. It pulled half way, reducing the snow and wind, but then it jammed. I yanked at it desperately until it closed.

The tent was still being buffeted by the wind outside, but inside there was now calm. I scrambled around on all fours, trying to brush the snow off everything and push it towards the tent entrance. There was an extraordinary amount of it. I was very, very cold, and bewildered as to what had just happened.

After what seemed like an eternity, but was probably a matter of seconds, I heard voices shouting outside the tent.

I cautiously unzipped the tent a small way and powdery snow collapsed inwards. The tent was buried by snow. It pushed in on every side, blotting out the sunlight.

I scraped the snow out of my way and stood up to survey

the chaos that was, less than two minutes before, a fully functioning and active expedition site. Now it looked like a war zone, as if it had been ransacked, pillaged by the Vikings.

I heard shouting cut across the windswept silence. "Everybody to the white pod!" the voice yelled. "Get in the white pod! Everybody to the white pod!"

I pulled my wet boots on over my sodden, frozen socks, not even bothering to do up the laces. I grabbed my downing jacket, shook the snow off it and cannoned out of the tent, taking a direct path to the white dome that rose above the surrounding tents.

I burst into the pod to find myself face-to-face with Bill, 'the highest chef in the world'. Only Bill was not his usual cheery self at all. It turned out that he had been standing in the open when the avalanche struck, with nowhere to run or hide. He'd ducked down in the snow to protect himself, and had been lucky enough to avoid any of the flying debris. But he was soaking wet – absolutely soaking wet – covered from head to toe in snow, his glasses had gone and he was standing there in total shock.

He didn't say a word. As we tended to him, he just stood motionless, as if his expression had been frozen on to his face by the cold of the avalanche.

I offered him a fizzy drink from the counter, knowing it might take the edge off the shock slightly. He didn't respond, or make any indication that he understood.

We sat him down and found him an extra pair of trousers to get him warmer and, soon after, he started to regain his composure. He started saying, over and over again, in a steadily stronger voice, "I'm OK, I'm OK, I'm OK..." as if he was trying to reassure himself. He was clearly in shock.

"There's been a huge avalanche," I heard a voice say, idiotically, and we all sat there in stunned silence, not knowing what to do next. People had scratches, scrapes, small cuts, but, miraculously, our expedition team had managed to get away without any major injuries. We soon discovered that others were not so lucky.

"What's going on? What's going on?" said Bill, as his shock gave way to curiosity.

Nobody knew.

We decided we needed to find out how the impact had affected the rest of camp and, as a mountain first aider, I volunteered to help the injured. I could deal with broken arms, broken legs, small injuries, that sort of thing. I was hoping I would be able to manage the situation until paramedics arrived in the next half an hour.

We didn't realise that nobody was coming. The only help up there comes via helicopter, and no helicopter was coming. We were alone.

When the earthquake hit, it loosened all the ice on top of Pumori, about a kilometre above us. Thousands of tons of ice had then come crashing down the mountain towards our fragile camp, gaining speed and power all the way. As it sped down the side of Pumori, it created a vacuum, which was released like a shotgun when it piled into the valley floor.

Because of the horseshoe shape of Pumori, the snow, ice

and rock were channelled towards us, increasing the power of the avalanche as it was unable to expand outwards. As it got to the edge of the horseshoe, it suddenly released itself and shot across the valley. Of course, that's exactly where we were. It just exploded across the middle of Base Camp and wiped everything out.

The destruction in our camp was quite unbelievable. Even though our expedition had got off lightly, due to our position slightly further away from Pumori, there was still a huge amount of damage. Our toilet tent had been completely destroyed, as had the tent of the expedition leader – who was, luckily for him, in Kathmandu at the time. The communications tent had also been completely destroyed, as if it had never existed in the first place. Both tents had been on a raised piece of ground.

Camping equipment – tent poles, clothing, boots – littered the ground, and large rocks had been displaced and chucked about the place like pebbles. Just one of those through your tent would have been enough to punch your ticket.

The poles from the toilet tent had shot through the air like spears, piercing the white pod like paper. We could see them sticking through the canvas three metres up. Even if I had rammed a tent pole with all my force into the canvas of the white pod, I couldn't have pierced it like that. Its canvas was extremely strong, so the force and speed that carried the poles must have been extraordinary.

It occurred to me how lucky I was to be unhurt.

While some of our expedition remained in the white pod,

others of us went out to see if we could help. We met one of the other larger expeditions, IMG, who told us it was far worse than we had thought. They told us there were many injured people, with lots of them urgently needing medical attention.

The plan was to make their mess tent into a temporary first aid/hospital tent. Any injured people would be sent there, while our white pod would be the tent where those who were unhurt could come for shelter, tea and biscuits and company.

Angelica, our expedition doctor, went to oversee the care of the injured in the other party's tent. Louise, our climbing heart surgeon, went with her.

Things didn't turn out according to this initial plan, however.

I made my way up to the ridges on the outskirts of our expedition's camp, to let people know they could get shelter and tea in our white pod. Woody, one of the guides, was up there too. We were stunned by what we saw.

The avalanche had hit the middle area of Base Camp with its full force, destroying *everything* in its path. Tents were torn to pieces, belongings were thrown hundreds of metres into the Icefall, electronic equipment including 12-volt car batteries (used to power lights) were thrown about like rag dolls. The relative order of Base Camp only minutes before had been turned into a chaotic spaghetti of confusion and disarray.

Some areas of the camp ground were completely destroyed, with piles of snow covering everything. I dreaded to think what had happened to the people in those tents.

People were rushing about, to and fro, seemingly without much purpose, like ants when their nest has been disturbed.

There was shouting, panic in the air, confusion.

A couple approached me, looking infinitely out of place in the destruction. At first, I couldn't place what was so odd about them, but then it hit me – they were wearing shorts. In this environment, this frozen wasteland, they were wearing shorts.

"We've got to go," the woman said.

"Yeah, yeah, I know, we've got to go, we've got to go," the man responded, eyes darting around chaotically in his panic.

As they came towards me, I went to stop them. I wasn't sure where they were planning to go, but dressed how they were, with one backpack between the pair of them; it didn't seem like a good idea.

"I'm not quite sure how bad things are," I said, "but there's a white pod down there. We've got some hot tea and biscuits. Why don't you come down and have a cup of tea?"

It didn't seem as though they had heard me. They definitely hadn't processed the information. The woman looked at me as if *I* was the one talking crazy.

"We've got to go, we've got to go," she repeated again. "We've got to go, to go down the valley."

They were terrified. Panic had set in and they were acting on their instinct to flee. I tried to reason with them – explaining that it was likely that the situation would be even worse down the valley, that supplies might be cut off, that they were in serious danger of catching frostbite without the proper equipment – but they couldn't be reasoned with.

The woman shouted again, "We've got to go, we've got to

go." That was all she could say.

They stumbled away through the snow and chaos, down the valley towards Gorak Shit. I never saw them again.

We heard from somewhere that the avalanche had been caused by a huge earthquake, greater than Richter force 8, and that its epicentre was close to Kathmandu. That couple was heading straight towards the centre of the madness, not away from it!

I thought back to my time in Kathmandu, before heading up the Khumbu Valley to Everest – the tiny, winding streets, the towering, tilting old buildings, the intricate spider webs of electrical wires strung along every street. I couldn't imagine much of that standing up to the pressures of an earthquake. How many people would be buried under the rubble? It was an awful thought. I couldn't think of anywhere more dangerous to go just then.

Logic, however, is a fickle thing, and it has a habit of evading us when we need it the most, when we are in the most difficult situations. Our instinct is flight.

This pair was not alone. There were streams of people heading for the exit, half-dressed, ill-prepared, in a mass exodus out of Base Camp. People were shouting, some were covered in blood, and as the afternoon dragged on, oblivious to the chaos within it, the daylight was fading fast.

Panic had set in, but I couldn't let it panic me. I had to think logically. I was safer at Everest Base Camp than I would be halfway down the Khumbu Valley. My kit was relatively intact, I had no injuries, there were people around me who needed help. Thoughts of reaching the summit had to be put on hold for the time being, but there was no way I was leaving the camp.

I saw the two girls from Adventure Consultants, Katherine and Angela, who had been part of our drinking party the night before.

Angela was the camp manager for Adventure Consultants. Katherine was from New Zealand, and had been employed as a personal physiotherapist for a millionaire who was attempting to reach the summit. Everest Base Camp was as far as she was expected to go.

She saw me, recognised me and made a beeline for me, her eyes wide with shock. She was covered in something dark, shimmering; it looked just as if she'd spilled some blackcurrant squash all over herself, all over her jacket. But it was blood, someone's blood. She came up and flung her arms around me, collapsing against me and sobbing and shaking uncontrollably, crying her eyes out.

Next to me, Angela hugged Woody; they both gripped on to us as if their lives depended on it.

Katherine shook in my arms, sobbing hysterically, burying her face in my jacket.

"It was awful. It was awful, awful," she said, between gasps for air. "Awful."

I'd never seen anything quite like it – someone who had just completely emotionally lost it. She was sobbing like a baby, shaking like a leaf. She was absolutely terrified.

After a short while, I suggested we go to the white pod for

some hot tea. I escorted both women back there, hoping the tea and company might calm them.

We learned that their camp had been hit the hardest, with the full force of the avalanche, as it crashed down off Pumori. There was nothing left of it at all. It was absolutely decimated, every tent ripped to shreds; the whole camp completely flattened.

Over hot tea, the two girls told us what had happened to them.

They were the only two Westerners from their expedition still at Base Camp. The rest of the Adventure Consultants expedition team, about 30 of them, were on rotation and had gone up to Everest Camp 1. We had no idea how they were or even if any of them were still alive, as there were no communications working.

When the avalanche hit, the two women had been outside the mess tent with three of their Sherpas, but close enough to use the mess tent for cover. They'd rushed in and dived on to the floor, awaiting the impact like everyone else at Base Camp.

The force of the avalanche had flattened the mess tent – it flattened every tent in the Adventure Consultants' campsite – and the pair of them were trapped within the tent, under the snow and ice.

When Katherine came to her senses, she could see a small pinprick of light, which she crawled towards; it was the only thing she could think of to do. She was buried under a pile of heavy items – chairs, tables, even the canvas tent – which was in turn covered in snow. It was slow, tough going, but she eventually reached the surface. She was extremely lucky that none of those flying objects had smashed directly into her.

After she had managed to crawl out, she found the camp manager, who had also successfully freed herself.

The three Sherpas, on the other hand, had dashed into the Sherpa mess tent, which was just beside the Westerners' mess tent. This was where they cooked for everyone, so it contained heavy cooking equipment, such as ovens and sinks.

Katherine had seen one of the Sherpas buried in the snow, and run over, still dizzy from the avalanche, to see if she could help him. Before she reached him, however, she stopped short with horror, falling to her knees in the snow.

The back of his head was completely smashed In. There was nothing left; it was all blood, red, matted, glistening on the white snow.

She kneeled down and put her arms around him and he looked into her eyes as she cradled him in her arms, holding him close as his blood oozed out and soaked her jacket. He soon died.

Both women tried to dig him out of the snow with their bare hands. They wanted to move his body away from the devastation a little. The cold bit at them mercilessly.

When they finally pulled his body clear, they discovered, like some new sick torment, the body of another Sherpa buried underneath him. They soon realised he was already dead. They found the third Sherpa a short distance way, also dead. The three men had been huddled together, trying to avoid all the heavy metallic equipment that must have been flying around in their tent.

All three Sherpas had been killed; miraculously the girls had survived. Their tents had been less than 10 metres apart. Survival was purely a matter of luck, of being in the right place at the right time...or rather, not being in the wrong place at the wrong time.

Katherine was confused, terrified – she couldn't quite grasp what was going on and was thinking about her loved ones back home. She wanted desperately to leave, to get back to her boyfriend.

Angela was coping better – she had been at Base Camp the year before, when 16 Sherpas had died in the Icefall, and the expeditions had been cancelled after the other Sherpas staged a strike. She soon headed out to see what she could do to help others.

I, too, went back outside. It was clear that there was still no communication, or any central management of the situation. Everyone was wandering around aimlessly. It was complete chaos.

There was blood everywhere, splattered on stones and snow like thick paint. People were staggering about as if someone had just detonated a bomb.

I made my way towards the mess tents to try to find out what was going on.

The emergency tent

As I pulled back the flap of our mess tent, I was immediately overwhelmed by a thick, metallic stench. It was a sickly smell, almost like treacle, but mixed with the unmistakable odour of blood and sweat. Not normal sweat, from exercise or heat, but the sweat of intense fear. It clung to the air like a disease, damp and claggy. It was the smell of death.

I took a deep breath, and stepped inside.

There were injured people everywhere – some seated, some lying on the floor – there was no semblance of organisation at all. I couldn't believe it. Nobody was doing anything to help the injured; they were just sitting there, looking frightened – or lying unconscious.

My immediate instinct was to try to bring some order to the chaos.

As I walked in, I was fighting my way past tables and chairs.

I got someone to help me move all the unwanted tables and chairs outside. We had to carry them carefully around the injured and dying bodies. Someone else held the flap of the tent open so that we could get through with them.

As I ducked outside, I took a huge breath of fresh air. It truly stank inside – blood, sweat, urine, fear, bleach. Why bleach? We didn't have any bleach… I had noticed the smell in hospitals, but always assumed it was the bleach they cleaned everything with. It must have been a scent bodies give off when they're dying.

Once we had taken a few tables out, we had space to start to get people to lie down, to make them comfortable and to get things sorted out a little. It went through my mind that perhaps somebody else was already actually in charge, and that I had just come in and trodden on their toes. I expected at any moment that someone would tap me on the shoulder and ask me to step out of the way. But it seemed better to do something than nothing.

I recalled the story of the woman who fell down a well in England. The fire brigade came and lowered a chap in to check on her. He pronounced that she had broken her leg and needed to be winched out and taken to hospital, but that she was conscious and generally in good health.

The head fireman said the winch could only support one person, so health and safety regulations meant they could not risk two people on it, and as the woman was not trained in the winch process (health and safety regulations again) she could not be allowed to go on it by herself.

He had to call his boss. After locating his boss an hour later, they got the reply that he wasn't sure either, because of health and safety concerns, and that he would need to contact the area manager.

Another hour went by and still the woman was down the well, and starting to suffer from hypothermia along with the broken leg. The area manager was not sure because of health and safety issues, and by this time, the media was interested, so everybody was afraid to make a decision, in case something went wrong and they got blamed after the event.

So they decided not to take any action until they could get a bigger winch in. Several hours later, a bigger winch arrived and the woman was lifted out. By now she was suffering from acute hypothermia. She later died in hospital.

This story was a fair warning to me of the perils of inaction. That smell, though...

Those people in the worst conditions in that tent were clearly fearing for their lives. They knew the severity of the conditions at Base Camp – they'd been here for weeks now. They knew it was a tough enough environment to survive in when you're in peak physical condition, but with the temperature plummeting to -15°C at night, and with injuries and loss of blood, they must have been petrified that they would not last the night.

I made my way around from casualty to casualty, checking each person over, assessing them and making a rudimentary attempt to prioritise their injuries. There was very little I could do, but I checked if they were conscious, if they were aware of where they were – I held up fingers and asked them to tell me how many, checked if they knew their names and where they were from. I thought their responses would at least let me know who was in a serious condition, who required immediate medical attention.

I dished out painkillers to whoever needed them, which was virtually everybody. Lincoln had provided me with a bucketload of blue tablets in a clear plastic bag, which he told me were Paracetamol. I wasn't about to question him at this point; the situation was so dire.

After the assessment and treatment for pain, I asked those with minor injuries to go to the white pod. It was now time for phase two – to organise the space properly, so that we could get more people lying down, and arrange them so that we could access them all without tripping over anyone. It really was that chaotic.

I asked the people sitting on chairs in the middle of the tent – most of whom had head injuries – if they would like to lie down.

"No," one of them said, in a strong Nepalese accent.

"No problem..." I paused – we had people coming in with more severe injuries. "We need to make more space. Do you think you could move to the side of the tent? We can do it slowly and I can help you." I wanted to keep the middle clear. They obliged, with some assistance.

More bodies were still coming in – a flow of confused, injured folk looking for some sort of help. We didn't have the facilities to cope with them all. They were supposed to be going to the IMG tent, not ours. We were supposed to be taking the non-injured in our camp, and we had only one doctor – Taka – on site.

What could I do? I couldn't exactly send them away and say we couldn't help them. Some of them could barely walk; some had no idea where they were.

Our expedition had two mess tents that seated 18 each

on a long table down the middle. These ended up serving as makeshift hospital tents. Both became full, with approximately 25 injured people crammed into the small space, and barely enough room to move between them.

Taka was looking after the injured people in the other tent, so it was left to me to take charge in the one I was in. I had to work out where my limited medical skills could make the greatest impact.

I rolled up my sleeves, took a deep breath and got stuck in. I wasn't feeling 100 per cent, but I had to put that to one side for now and focus on the task in hand. I had to try to keep these people alive until help arrived...whenever that might be.

I knew by now that the avalanche had been caused by a huge earthquake. Some expeditions had satellite phones and had managed to make calls, and news had flowed in that the earthquake had devastated large areas of Nepal, so the helicopters would be drafted to help with rescue operations. I had no idea if the casualties on top of Everest were a high priority – or even if they were a priority at all – so there was no telling how long we would have to make do and deal with the casualties ourselves, with no real medical supplies, in freezing, unforgiving conditions.

I put those thoughts out of my mind. Taka and I needed to work together. The trouble was, he spoke very little English, and I didn't speak a word of Japanese, so communication was very difficult. The other Japanese member of our expedition – Hachiro – acted as interpreter, enabling us to converse in a rudimentary way.

I told Taka who was the most injured, who concerned me the most, and he checked everyone over once more. We discussed the injuries – we only had Ibuprofen and Paracetamol, so there was a limited amount we could do. Once we had discussed everybody, he returned to his tent to care for his patients.

It was basically up to me from that point.

By the time I had completed the initial assessment of everybody, organised the tent, and done what I could with Taka, bandages and painkillers, three hours had passed since the avalanche. Many people had either left BC, or come to our expedition camp or IMG's. The flow of bodies had slowed right down.

I remembered I had promised to check on Katherine. I asked one of the other expedition members to take charge for five minutes while I nipped back to the white pod to see her.

She was still sitting, looking blankly into space, rocking slightly to and fro. I took her hand in mine, explaining, that I was busy with the wounded and asked if she would be all right.

"Yeah, I'm fine, I'm fine. Don't worry."

I didn't realise, at the time, that she would wake up every night, screaming, clawing in the darkness at some unknown spectre. From across the campsite, in the dead of night, we'd hear a shrill scream cut into the silence, followed by sobbing and crying. It was horrific – I don't know that she'll ever fully recover from what she saw.

I made my way back to the mess tent, blocking out the immediate chaos that surrounded me, knowing that I was in it for the long haul.

I turned the small gas heater on in an attempt to keep the injured warm. It was now the dreaded 4pm, and the temperature was plummeting. We only had a limited amount of fuel, so rationing the heat was very important. Luckily, as every person at Everest Base Camp was prepared for adverse weather conditions, there was no shortage of downing climbing gear and downing sleeping bags available. We collected as many as we could from the nearby area.

Soon after, a group of Sherpas arrived, carrying what appeared to be a camp bed. They were quiet, very sombre, and there was no noise coming from the shape on the bed.

Half of those in the tent, for all their injuries and ailments, were in strong voice – they moaned and groaned and continually asked for water. This, I knew, was a good sign – a moaning patient is a very conscious patient. This was infinitely reassuring to me, as I knew their injuries were less likely to be life-threatening.

The quietness, stillness of this camp bed was disconcerting. The Sherpas carrying it in seemed to be acting almost like pallbearers.

On the bed, wrapped in an array of camping equipment, was another Sherpa. His body seemed to lie with an unusual flatness, his limbs limp and lifeless.

His eyes were sunken, unreflective, without the usual spark of life, and his breathing was very laboured and stilted, the air rattling in his lungs uselessly.

I knew there was very little I could do – I had some bandages, painkillers, plasters; I could maybe make a rudimentary splint for a broken arm. He was too weak to swallow anything.

His left arm and lower body were soaked in blood. It was impossible in the dim light of the tent to determine the true extent of his injuries, but I knew it was bad.

I decided we should try to keep him warm, and see if we could get some fluid into his body.

I asked the kitchen to prepare some flasks of warm water, which I then poured into a plastic mug, making sure it was not too hot.

I asked one of the Sherpas who had brought the injured man in to pour a few drops on his lips very, very slowly. I checked that he understood what I meant – he nodded, took the cup and gently lowered it onto the man's lips.

A short while later, I felt a tugging at my sleeve and turned to face the Sherpa I had just spoken to. He clutched the plastic mug and pointed over to his friend.

I rushed over – the man's eyes had rolled back and he had stopped breathing. I felt his neck for a pulse. There was nothing. He was dead. He died in my mess tent, wrapped in sleeping bags, on a camp bed at Everest Base Camp. I never knew his name, where he came from or anything about him. I was in his company for less than five minutes, in which time he breathed his last breath and departed from this world.

I felt a sudden wave of nausea wash over me at the sheer desperation of the situation. These people were depending on me and I had very little to give – no real medical supplies, no bandages, no syringes, no real medicine. I felt as though I was going to cry.

"Pull yourself together, you idiot," I muttered, and slapped myself hard.

It must have been a very strange sight for the Sherpas – their friend had just died, and this crazed Westerner was slapping himself around the face.

I closed the dead Sherpa's eyes, pulling the sleeping bag over his head.

The Sherpas who had carried him in, and those who had followed, surrounded his body and began to chant. A low, rumbling chant with a haunting, ghostly tone.

The injured people in the tent began looking over, fear glinting in their eyes – many seemed in that specific moment to realise the true severity of the situation.

"What are you doing?" I asked one of the Sherpas.

The Sherpas have a very strict and traditional rite of passage – the ceremony is very particular. At the time of death, the body should be washed and covered in a white shroud. A lock of the deceased's hair should be cut off so that the life breath of the departed can leave the body – the sacred texts are read and there is a lot of chanting.

I had every respect for their religious ceremony; I was well aware how important it must be to Sherpa culture. But I was also aware that my patients were beginning to become unnerved, and that was the last thing I needed.

I dashed out of the tent, grabbed the nearest person and explained that we needed to find somewhere for the Sherpas to do their prayer ceremony – somewhere that wasn't my hospital tent.

Next to the kitchen was a wash tent, about three metres by three metres in size. I asked the Sherpas if that would be a suitable place for them and they agreed, lifting the makeshift stretcher with its lifeless body out of the mess tent and away.

I heaved a sigh of relief – but it wasn't long before the next problem walked through the door.

I'd started to fear what would come through the entrance of the tent. I knew that, any second, somebody else might be carried in, clinging desperately to life, and there would be very little I could do.

It didn't take long for my fears to be realised.

A Sherpa, supported by two Westerners, each with an arm under his, was dragged into the tent. He was very dazed and confused, blood covering his jacket, his trousers; he was in a hell of a state. I couldn't actually see his face properly, roughly applied bandages covered half of it, including his right eye – the rest of it was covered in glistening blood.

His one visible eye seemed entirely vacant.

We sat him gently down, and I grabbed the nearest Sherpa, whom I knew was able to speak English. "Translate for me," I said. "Translate what I'm saying."

I started to ask where he was in the most pain and the Sherpa began to translate. The man's good eye half-focused on me.

"No…"

He wasn't a Sherpa at all. The blood was so thick on his face wherever it was not bandaged, that it was impossible to tell.

"What's your name?"

"Marr..."

"Mark?"

"Yeth..."

It was almost impossible to understand him. Blood began to seep out from under the bandages above his right eye.

He began to shake. He juddered and jerked uncontrollably as we stood over him.

I could see that he had lost so much blood that he was at risk of going into cardiac arrest, and if I didn't act quickly to try to prevent it, it would be too late.

When the avalanche had hit, Mark had been walking in the open, with no protective cover nearby. He'd been hit by the full force of the impact, thrown unceremoniously around by it. It was amazing that he was alive at all.

I didn't think he'd be alive much longer.

I ran to Taka for help.

Hachiro translated my message; it seemed to take an eternity.

All the while, blood was oozing out of the back of Mark's neck.

Finally Taka got the message and rushed through to see him.

Mark was wearing a big downing jacket with a high collar, originally intended to protect his face and neck from the cold. Now it pressed against his wounds, acting as a compress.

There was an intense smell coming off him – sort of like

fried pig, like bacon. The smell of his blood was almost overwhelming – he smelt like an abattoir. He continued to shake.

After Taka had quickly checked him over, we fashioned a splint for his neck out of a bit of polystyrene. We suspected he'd broken his neck, and any sudden movements could have been the end of him.

We duct-taped the polystyrene brace to his forehead and to his back as he sat in the chair.

"Where are you from?" I asked, doing my best to keep the panic out of my voice.

His breathing was shallow; he'd managed to control his shuddering slightly.

"Amsterrrrdammm," he said, in a voice barely more than a whisper.

He was very, very cold, with no shoes on, just socks. We had to warm him up and get some fluid inside him to counteract the large amount of blood he was losing.

"Can you swallow?" I asked him.

He couldn't. I wanted to get some Paracetamol into his system. I knew it wouldn't do much, but it might take the edge off the pain slightly.

What I didn't want was for him to jerk his head back in an attempt to swallow the tablets. There was severe damage to his neck, and if his vertebrae were broken, any violent movement could be fatal.

"Can you bite on these, crunch these up?"

There was a very faint nod and I pushed the blue Paracetamol

Waiting at Kathmandu airport for our flights to Lukla. As all expeditions go in April, it's hot, smelly and chaotic — but luxurious compared with what was to come. Inset: Everest route map

The narrow track we followed for 10 days up the beautiful Khumbu Valley — no roads up here

In the old climbing gear museum at the Namche Bazaar with its owner, who sold me the jacket

The yeti skull at Khumjung village monastery —
to see it, I had to cross the monk's palm with $5

Sherpa woman planting bok choy and potatoes.
What looks like white gloves is actually her skin

One of the lodges on the way up the Khumbu Valley. We all sat around the outside walls facing each
other, with the "help yourself" food on the central table — and an efficient Yak poo-burning stove

First sight of Everest — everybody got very excited and a little nervous

Seen on my return in 2016, this was a chilling reminder of how lucky I was to have survived

The Everest graveyard (memorials to all the climbers who never came back). This is en route to EBC — it gives shocking pause for thought on the dangers of the climb

This is how barren EBC is — my tent is the one on the left of the picture

What better way to spend down time? I was too out of breath to sing much, though

The EBC facilities — so nice to have a throne to sit on, rather than 'stand and drop'

On Pumori looking towards Everest. The yellow dots are our tents. The Icefall is left of my hat

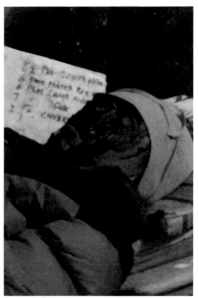

The temporary hospital. We put the injured into sleeping bags to survive the -15C night

Mark Rugal. When he came in, his face was so covered in blood that I thought he was a Sherpa

A picture I took the day after the earthquake and avalanche, showing the destruction the avalanche caused as it swept through Everest Base Camp, obliterating everything in its path

Another picture I took the day after the avalanche, showing the devastation at EBC

Figuring out how to reopen the kitchen after the avalanche

This is one of the most chilling pictures I took — four dead bodies we wrapped up in tent canvas

The devastation in Kathmandu. When the earthquake hit, many of the old buildings that were poorly constructed — like this one — just crumbled to the ground

Stairs in a Kathmandu supermarket — still in use, despite the damage, with business as usual

Last push for the summit in 2016 — I am the front one of the last three people in the photo

On the way down after summiting in 2016, between Camps 4 and 3, with the very steep Lotse face behind me. Inset: Me on top of the world – for those few minutes, the highest Mountain in the world

With my dear friend and Sherpa, Lakpa, at the foot of the Icefall, after summiting. Our expedition leader, Dr Nima, trekked up to meet us there with some beers. I have never enjoyed a beer so much

tablets into his mouth.

I had a cup of warm water, which I had to make sure was not too hot with my dirty finger. I didn't think he'd realise if he burned his mouth, let alone care.

I parted his lips for him – he could barely move them – and carefully poured a few drops of the water into his mouth. He gurgled slightly, as if he had no control over his neck muscles.

I froze, holding the cup next to his chapped and bloodied lips, praying he wouldn't choke.

The water passed and he continued his shallow, laboured breathing. His good eye looked up at me with thanks.

He would slurp some of the liquid, then slowly swallow it down, gasping all the while as if he was dying, like it was his dying breath. Every time he took some water, he gurgled – his throat was so dry.

It's amazing what the human body can endure – this man should not have been alive; he should have been dead. I think it was only his will that was keeping him going. I was terrified he'd fall off the chair and finish his neck off.

"We've got to get you lying down; we've got to get you flat."

I went out of the tent and shouted for a mattress and a sleeping bag. Time was of the essence, and the sooner I got Mark horizontal the better. I needed to make him as comfortable as it was possible to make someone in his state.

We made a space in the corner, moving chairs and bags out of the way.

"We're going to get you into a lying position – we're going to move you very slowly, OK?"

"Yeth," he said, through gritted teeth.

John and one of the Sherpas, who were assisting me, held Mark under the arms, taking most of his body weight, while I positioned myself behind his head to support his head and keep his neck still, to negate any movement as we lowered him.

It took the three of us quite some time to lower him gingerly on to a mattress, covering him in sleeping bags to try and get some warmth back into his very cold body.

When we had positioned him on the floor, we tucked thin, sponge pillows underneath his shoulders and head to help support his neck. It was a laborious process, slowly tucking each pillow in, one at a time, all the while trying to keep him as still as possible. His breath was very short; it was clear that lying down had been a hugely exhausting process for him.

"Jeepers," I thought, "this guy's never going to make it if we can't get him out of here, if we can't get him on to a helicopter." And yet moving him again was going to be highly risky too.

I knew for a fact there would be no helicopters coming that day, and the nearest hospital was in Lukla – ten day's trek away. No hope of Mark doing that, then. The only way to get him out was by helicopter, and with the avalanche and earthquake, no helicopter was likely to make it up to us anytime soon.

No one was coming to help us. We were all alone, stranded halfway up the highest mountain in the world, with the temperature starting to plummet towards -15°C. We were as far from civilisation as we could possibly be.

On the other hand, I realised it was actually a stroke of luck that there had been no helicopters at Base Camp at the time of the avalanche. A fragile chopper would have stood no chance against the force of the impact. It would have been decimated. The debris would have been even more dangerous – propeller blades, heavy electric equipment – so it might merely have added to the death toll.

"My theet... my theet," said Mark, through pursed lips.

"Your what?" I asked, bending over him and putting my ear to his lips.

"My theet."

I came back to my senses. His feet weren't in the sleeping bag; they were lying limply beside it.

I realised they were sodden wet. After the impact, he had stumbled around Base Camp with a possible broken neck and with no shoes on. How was he alive?

I got down on my knees and carefully removed the soaking wet socks, being careful not to jerk him.

His feet were like blocks of ice – they didn't feel like feet at all. The skin was hard, with an alien bluish hue that concerned me greatly. His blood had all gone to his core, naturally. His feet had inflated; they were bloated like puffer fish.

"We've got to warm his feet up, we've got to warm his feet up," I repeated in my head, over and over again.

If he caught frostbite, his already slim chances of survival would be effectively destroyed.

John was over on the other side of the tent, checking on some of the other patients. I beckoned him over, cautious of panicking Mark.

I whispered, "Can you see if you can get some socks for the injured? Just ask everybody in our expedition if we can borrow loads of clean socks."

After John left, I grabbed the small gas heater and positioned it about a foot away from Mark's feet. I didn't want to burn him – it was likely he wouldn't notice if I did anyway – but it was vital to slowly warm his feet back up again.

I kneeled over him like a monk at prayer, all the while breathing in that putrid smell of blood, sweat and fear.

"Can you feel that?" I asked, touching his feet.

He couldn't feel anything.

Any normal human could and would be unable to keep their skin in such close proximity to the gas heater for that length of time. The fact that he couldn't feel it at all concerned me greatly. He had clearly lost a lot of blood, and the rest had gone to his core... He was, in fact, dying.

John returned, clutching a mismatched array of hiking socks. The good thing about climbing types is that they always seem to carry an excessive amount of socks.

Carefully, we pulled two pairs of socks on to the frozen blocks of ice at the end of Mark's legs. I pulled the heater slightly closer.

"Can you feel that?" I asked again.

Nothing.

John and I exchanged concerned looks. In the best of situations, frostbite is a difficult condition to deal with. We were not in the best of situations; we didn't know what we were going to do.

"Can you feel that?" I said – I squeezed his sweaty, stinky feet with my blood-soaked hands. "Mark, can you feel that?"

"I can'th..." he began. I closed my eyes. "Yeth... yeth..."

He could feel something! That meant there was still some live tissue in his feet, that his feet weren't dead. That was the best possible news at that point.

We kept the heater on him for another five minutes or so as the feeling gradually returned, then we slid his freshly sock-covered feet into the sleeping bag and zipped it up about halfway – it wasn't possible to get it zipped all the way up without risking damage to his neck.

We got a second sleeping bag and put that over him as well, to try to keep him warm. We kept the gas heater nearby, blasting heat in his direction.

I think, without that heater, he would have lost his feet and probably his life.

For now though, he was reasonably stable. He was managing to breathe on his own, but I needed to get some fluid into him to replace the huge blood loss. I asked John if he could get a cup of warm water and very gently hold it to Mark's lips, and try to get Mark to swallow some without choking. If he choked, I was terrified it would finish off his neck.

I also asked a Sherpa if he could sit in the corner, near enough that Mark could see him at all times. The only way we'd been able to position him meant that he was facing the canvas of the back of the tent – I didn't want him to think we'd forgotten about him, or that he was all on his own. I wanted him to be able to see a human face whenever he opened his good eye, to know that we were still there for him if he should need us. I thought that terribly important for him. I thought it could help keep him alive.

He was so badly injured, so entirely dependent on my care, that it was like dealing with a small child – he was so grateful, so thankful for anything that I did to help ease his suffering.

Again, the canvas door of the tent opened. Again, I feared the worst.

A man entered, helped by two others, clutching his hands across his chest. He was clearly in a lot of pain, but appeared to be relatively coherent and was walking of his own accord.

He stood in the doorway, a little unsure. I approached him.

He was wearing an all-in-one downing summit suit, with the name 'Tony' typed on the front.

"Hi Tony," I said. "Are you alright?"

He stared at me, perplexed.

"I'm not Tony," he said.

"That's what it says on your jacket."

We all had downing suits, all-in-one jumpsuits, that we would wear only on summit day, when we trekked from Camp 3 to Camp 4 and from there to the summit.

When the avalanche had hit, this man had been relaxing in his tent in his pants and a T-shirt. The avalanche had ripped the tent off him and he'd lost everything. He was left out in the open, wearing nothing but his underwear and a T-shirt.

He wandered around in the snow in his socks, half-dazed, trying to find something – anything – to wear.

He came across a jumpsuit, splayed out in the snow like a corpse – another piece of debris discarded by the avalanche – and he pulled it on. He had no idea who 'Tony' was. That didn't matter at the time.

"I'm Richard," he said.

"I'm Jules."

I asked Richard what the problem was and he indicated that it was his chest.

I pulled the jumpsuit open to have a better look. The skin across his chest was a deep purple-brown colour, like rotten fruit.

I felt each rib gently and in the middle ribs Richard let out a sharp squeal of pain.

It was clear that he had broken his ribs, so I checked his stomach to see if the breaks had caused any collateral damage. Broken ribs we could deal with; a punctured stomach or lungs would be different.

"Mate, you're lucky," I told him. "You're actually fine. You've broken a couple of ribs, but that's all. It's going to hurt like hell, but that's it – you're going to be OK." This seemed greatly to reassure him, as per my intention.

The avalanche had launched him clear of his tent and he'd managed to walk away with only three broken ribs. It was nothing short of a miracle. Richard was a lucky guy – although he probably didn't feel it at the time.

I gave him some Paracetamol and a cup of warm water, which he swallowed thankfully, before I sat him on a chair.

"You'll have to keep as still as you can – no sudden

movements. There's nothing else we can give you to ease the pain."

I wondered how long it would be before we would see any evac choppers.

Richard groaned and grimaced as we helped him sit down, his eyes screwed up in pain. With any movement, the pain was very evident – he was one of the louder patients in the tent, but that reassured me that he was going to be fine.

"Jules, thank you... is there any food going?"

It had been a long time since breakfast. I mean, breakfast felt like a different life, a different universe – and it was now getting on for 4.30 in the afternoon.

I approached John. "People are beginning to get hungry," I said. "We need to feed them."

We called on Bill the chef, who knocked up a large amount of soup, which we could then distribute among the people in the mess tents.

Soon, there was silence save for the sounds of slurping and gurgling. Immediately after surviving a catastrophe, hunger isn't important – the body focuses itself on the more pressing issue of staying alive. But when you get to somewhere safe, when you're warm, when everything goes quiet, then hunger comes back with a vengeance.

Those who were able to move lapped the soup down like they hadn't eaten in days. This was great, because all of them, with the exception of Richard, had lost a considerable amount of blood. It was good that they were getting some warm fluid back into their bodies.

The more severely injured were not able to feed themselves.

Mark lay quietly in the corner, facing the canvas of the tent, not making a single sound or movement. We couldn't feed him any of the bits in the soup – the risk of his choking on them was too great, and there was no way we were going to risk sitting him upright again.

So, over the course of about half an hour, John fed Mark drop after drop of soup, sieving it, cooling it down and feeding it to him like a baby. All the while, Mark gurgled, thankful for the warmth it was bringing to his body.

The level of concentration this operation required was intense – John barely blinked the entire time, kneeling inches away from Mark's battered and bloody face. It was an impressive spectacle to behold. I'm sure Mark will never forget it; nor will John.

The tent door opened again.

A Gurkha captain stumbled in, blood seeping down the side of his head. He steadied himself.

"What happened?" I asked.

"We were coming out of the Icefall, coming down," he told me. "There were six of us; we were in the Icefall... We ran, we ran."

They were clipped into the rope that marked the route through the Icefall. The captain told me how one of the team got his karabiner stuck and couldn't move as the avalanche advanced on them.

The captain had unclipped from the rope and run. They were wearing crampons, which are unwieldy at the best of times, and impossible to run in.

He was trying to run, with the wall of snow, ice and rock hurtling along behind him, gaining all the time. Something struck him in the side of the head. He remembered nothing more.

The Gurkha captain was wearing a beanie hat, which I attempted to remove to see the damage to his head.

The blood had matted and congealed, sticking the hat to his head. I decided it was better to leave it on – removing it would only re-open the wound and could do further damage, and I had no bandages left. At the very least, the beanie hat would keep his head warm, and it was no longer bleeding.

I had no bandages, no plastic gloves – my hands were covered in blood already.

He seemed *compos mentis* enough. I felt confident he wasn't in any immediate danger.

"Thank you, thank you," he said, as I seated him and gave him some Paracetamol and warm water and soup. "Is there anything to eat?"

I nipped out to ask Bill if there was anything a bit more solid than the soup that we could give to patients who weren't so ill and who could still eat.

He whipped up a meal of rice and potatoes and brought it through in two large cauldrons, which we put just inside the mess tent, along with some bowls. We were then able to dish it out to those who wanted to eat.

Very few actually wanted any. Most people were still fairly consumed by their injuries and couldn't focus on eating rice and potatoes – the soup had been enough.

Another member of the Gurkha regiment entered the tent and approached me, asking if he could stay with his captain.

I had cleared every other non-essential person out by this point. Everybody who was not injured had been asked to leave. Just John and I remained, taking care of the patients.

"You can stay," I said to the Gurkha, "but you need to help me if I need you."

He agreed to this, pulling up a chair next to the captain.

There seems to be great camaraderie among the Gurkhas.

We now had a team of three, a skeleton crew tasked with the care of all these people. It was starting to get late, the light was failing rapidly, and as it did so the temperature began to plummet.

I needed a breath of fresh air for two minutes.

I stepped outside. Stopping, taking a second to think about what was actually happening, I could feel it all welling up inside me.

I walked round to the side of the tent, out of sight. I just wanted to blub, to cry. From being around so much pain, suffering and death in one place for that extended period of time...a very cold feeling came over me.

"Stop it," I told myself out loud. "Get a grip, get a grip. These people need help; they need you to support them in whatever little way you can."

I slapped myself across the face again.

"Get a grip."

I slapped myself once more, talking to myself like some sort of madman.

"Get a grip, get a grip, get a grip."

I took a deep breath, pushed all other thoughts to the back of my mind, suppressed the horror and fear that was threatening to stop me from doing what I needed to do.

I stopped myself from thinking about anything but the task in hand, and focused on getting on with it. I needed to bury myself in the middle of it to avoid having to look at it properly.

I took a few more deep breaths, focusing on the depth of my breathing – in, out, in, out – then I stepped back into the tent, as if nothing had happened.

The next task was getting these people prepared for the night. We needed to get them all lying down and as comfortable as possible.

I stepped out of the tent and called for more mattresses and sleeping bags. I also suggested to Taka and Hachiro, whose charges were mostly less seriously injured than those we were caring for, that we move all their more serious cases into our tent, while the less seriously injured should head to the white pod for the night. That way, we could manage all the seriously injured in one tent, which would make it easier for the four of us – John, myself, Taka and Hachiro – to get at least some rest, as only one of us would need to be on duty at a time. Each of us could do a three-hour shift while the others slept.

We would also get one mess tent back to feed our expedition team, and uninjured people from other expeditions. It was very important that the uninjured stayed well and healthy, so they could help look after the injured.

This plan meant, however, that my tent would be full to the brim.

It was a major logistical process, trying to fit enough mattresses into the tent for all the injured people. This was not a neat, tidy hospital ward with everything in its place. It was a makeshift, chaotic emergency room; the result of a hundred spur-of-the-moment decisions. We had to move patients around, stand them up or shift them from chair to chair while we got the mattresses in place. The floor was also littered with people's bags, coats, hiking equipment. John and I unceremoniously chucked out everything that wasn't vital. We would place a mattress, find a sleeping bag, ease a patient into it and then move on to the next mattress, the next patient.

Two people wanted to stay sitting up, rather than lying down: the Gurkha captain, who was now in good spirits, and a Sherpa with very bad injuries – we suspected he had a broken arm, broken collarbone and a lot of broken ribs. Every time he moved, even a few inches, he was clearly in excruciating agony. The thought of lying down must have filled him with dread.

"I want to sit up," he kept saying. We made him as comfortable as we could.

Richard, who sat with the face of a man in constant pain, also needed to be helped to lie down. I called the Gurkha who was assisting me. We carefully placed our hands under Richard's arms and helped him to a standing position. He groaned loudly as we lifted him upright.

We moved his chair and put a mattress on the floor by the

entrance to the tent. We got a sleeping bag, opened it right out – the plan was to lower him onto it and then wrap the sleeping bag around him.

We lowered him slowly. A jarring, grinding cracking noise escaped from his chest – the sound of the break scraping as he moved. He let out an almighty scream of pain.

We could feel the cracked ribs opening and closing as we lowered him. He screamed in pain again.

We managed to get him into a sitting position, tucking his legs into the sleeping bag and positioning pillows behind him.

"I'm not comfortable," he said. "Mate, I'm not comfortable."

What a performance it was!

We pulled his leg a bit, moved the other leg around, then the first one again. We had to move everything for him, because every time he tried to move himself he would pull his ribs.

Finally, we got him lying flat. He screamed as his ribs cracked back into position. He still wasn't at ease. We shunted him about, and then his jumpsuit wasn't comfortable, so we had to move that down. It took an age to sort things out to the best of our ability so that he could rest for the night.

"Thank you, thank you, thank you," he kept saying. His extreme appreciation for what we were trying to do was very touching. I felt very emotional. I just wanted to burst into tears. So much appreciation for what I considered to be the minimum anyone who could would have done for him.

I had to turn away and slap myself again.

"Get a grip."

I told myself I could do all the blubbing I wanted in the

morning – I could lose the plot then – but not now, not here, not when I was actually needed.

I wasn't sure how long I was going to be able to keep going, keep pushing down and subduing all the negative thoughts. I would need a break soon.

I had already heard that a weather front was coming in, and that it was expected to last three days, so no helicopters would be able to reach us. Potentially, then, we would be looking after everybody for the next three days... The thought filled me with dread.

I organised the night shifts, with myself taking the first shift, from nine o'clock until midnight, followed by John, then Taka and then Hachiro. We would be able to make clearer decisions in the cold (and it would be cold) light of day. I didn't know what we were going to do, how long we were going to have to keep playing at being doctors. We would cross that bridge when we came to it.

Before I could begin my shift I needed some food. I asked John to look after everyone for a while and made my way to the mess tent. There was nobody and no food in there. I wondered into the kitchen tent and found Bill.

"We've cleared up, I'm afraid," he said. My heart sank. I was so hungry, so exhausted. "But if you go to the Sherpas' tent, they might have something."

I thanked him and turned to look at the steep hill I had to climb to reach the Sherpas' tent. I was completely exhausted. I plodded very slowly up the hill of ice and stones – I felt as if I were climbing Everest itself.

The Sherpas had a slightly different diet to the Westerners – mainly vegetarian, as meat is prized and very expensive for them – but they were kind enough to give me some rice, potatoes and *dal bhat*. They were just about to clear up, but they dumped a huge pile of food on a plate for me.

I scrubbed the dried blood and sweat off my hands and bolted down the food, chasing it with cup after cup after cup of lemon tea. I barely tasted any of it, but the warmth was nourishment enough.

Twenty minutes later, I was back in my hospital mess tent with John, ready to begin my solo vigil.

John left and the tent instantly became eerily quiet. The rush and panic, the cacophony of groans, grunts and yells, all evaporated like ice in the desert.

I found a sleeping bag and mattress for the Gurkha who had agreed to assist me. The deal was that he could stay in the tent with his captain, but I could wake him up to help me during the night when needed.

I sat down in a chair, zipped up my downing jacket and turned on my head torch. There was a source of light in the mess tent from a very low-energy bulb powered by a car battery that had been linked to a solar panel, but it was so dim that the bodies wrapped up in the sleeping bags seemed more and more like corpses in a morgue. The light from the head torch brought me some comfort in the darkness.

My mind started to wander, sticking cruelly on thoughts about the horrors of the day. I thought about Mark, the Gurkha captain, I heard Richard's cries of pain, I thought of the limp, lifeless corpse of the Sherpa whose name I would never know.

I thought about the blood on my hands.

If I'd sat there for three hours, just thinking, the weight of my reflections would have crushed me before long. I would have gone mad.

I decided I would read my book for a while, so I woke up the Gurkha and told him to keep an eye on everybody while I went to my tent and grabbed my copy of *Many Years From Now*, the biography of Paul McCartney, which I had been thumbing idly throughout my time at Base Camp, without too much engagement.

Now, however, the option to teleport myself into the surreal world of The Beatles was heaven. It was like an oasis for my mind, transporting me away from the horror of what I had witnessed.

It would prove to be only brief respite.

As I sat like a WW1 matron surrounded by my patients in the mess tent, reading, my eyelids started to get heavy. Keeping them open became a difficult challenge. It became almost impossible to focus on the words as they blurred and distorted on the page, skipping about capriciously.

Then, from out of the darkness: "Jules, mate, mate, mate..."

My eyes sprang open, suddenly unburdened by the tiredness that had seemed omnipotent only seconds before. Was it seconds before? What time was it?

I looked down at my watch, my head torch illuminating the dial.

21.33.

"Jules, are you there?"

I looked around for the source of the voice, shining light on body after body; sometimes I'd catch a glint, a reflection from an open pair of ghostly eyes, like cats in the shadows.

"Jules, over here."

It was Richard. He lay on his back, propped up absurdly by an array of mismatched pillows.

"What's wrong?" I asked.

"Have you got any more painkillers? It's hurting like..." he let out a small groan.

I knelt down, put my hand behind his neck and lifted his head gently and gave him two more of the blue tablets. I knew roughly when they'd all had their last dose, so I wasn't too concerned about giving them more.

I held a cup of warm water to his mouth and he swallowed the pills.

"Thanks mate," he said, as I laid his head back down on the pillows.

I returned to the solace of The Beatles.

"Jules?" Richard's voice again.

I made my way back over, taking care to avoid stepping on the sleeping lions along the way.

"I need to go to the toilet. Sorry mate."

I hadn't really considered this. I looked about at all the people in the tent... Jeepers, if they all wanted to pee, this was going to be a nightmare.

I went over to the Gurkha who had stayed with his captain and shook him awake.

"I need your help."

I put my arm behind Richard's neck.

"We're going to get you into a seated position – this is going to hurt a bit mate, but try not to make too much noise and wake the others."

Together, we slowly lifted him up into a seated position. I could hear his ribs pop – he let out a whimper of pain.

The beams from our head torches darted around the room as we moved.

"We're now going to lift you into a standing position, and this is going to hurt again," I said. "You are going to feel this a lot."

We locked our arms under his and lifted him slowly to his feet. Richard wasn't a small guy – he was at least six foot – and his entire weight was on us. We hauled him up with everything we had.

He yelped with pain.

"Shh! Everybody else is sleeping – you've got to try to keep the noise down," I said.

Richard accepted this information with no argument – he was as exhausted as the rest of us.

He was now standing – swaying – held upright by the Gurkha.

I fetched a green plastic washing-up bowl that had been discarded in the corner of the tent.

"I'll hold this for you," I said. "Can you pee into it?"

Richard said he could. He grimaced, clearly in a lot of pain.

I held the bowl.

He managed to do the rest, thankfully. We looked away, as if privacy was a major concern at this point, as if anybody really cared about that any more, as if we were still civilised.

Once he had finished, I set the bowl down on the floor and we began the laborious process of lying him down again.

I heard his ribs crack again – the pain would be terrible – but his yells of pain were more subdued, forcing their way out from behind clenched teeth.

We got him back into his sleeping bag.

He then slept peacefully for the rest of the night – which was a relief.

I took the bowl of steamy pee out of the tent and threw it into the snow outside.

As I moved slowly back across the tent to my chair, to the escapism of The Beatles, there was a rustling among the bodies.

The noise of Richard had evidently woken up one of the injured Sherpas.

"Pee pee," he said. "I need pee pee."

The Sherpas, as a general rule, don't tend to wash as much as the Westerners while up Everest. They see it as an unnecessary luxury, I suppose.

I approached the Sherpa to help him, and the stench of his clothing was almost overwhelming. It smelt like rotten cabbages, sweaty socks and dried blood.

I put that to one side: here was a man in need of help, an injured human being who needs the help of another human being.

His injuries were far worse than Richard's. He had some kind of head wound, and was as pale as anything.

I teamed up with the Gurkha again; we lifted the Sherpa to his feet. I held the green washing-up bowl and looked away.

Richard, who wasn't suffering from any head injuries and who had complete control of his mind, was fairly accurate. The same could not be said of the Sherpa – whether due to his injuries or the fact that he just didn't care anymore, I don't know, but the result wasn't pretty.

After he had finished, there was some pee in the bowl, some down his leg, over his sleeping bag, and over my bloodied hand.

There was no way we were going to be able to dry him off – we didn't even have the facilities for *that*. We didn't even have the facilities to wash – so we had to hope that the warmth from the heater would do the job for us.

We packed him back in his sleeping bag and he drifted off for the night.

How many more times were we going to have to go through the peeing process? It was exhausting.

I went back to my chair.

Time crept onwards; it seemed ever more reluctant to move forward, the closer to midnight it got.

At 11:30, I was almost daring to think about bed – sleeping in my coffin tent seemed like a lavish treat to me at that point.

"Julsh?"

The last voice I hoped to hear. It cut through the murky silence like a knife.

"Yes, Mark?"

"I neeth the toileth."

Shit. What's the golden rule about people with neck injuries – keep them very still to avoid more damage. But I had to do something – I couldn't let him pee his pants. This was going to be a major frigging operation. It really required three people – one to hold his head and neck, while the other two took the weight of his body.

Shit.

I thought about rolling him on to his side to pee, but I feared this could prove fatal, so I decided the easiest thing to do was to lift him straight up, keeping his head still.

I woke the Gurkha again. I could see from the look on his face that he was thinking the same as I was.

I unzipped Mark's sleeping bag.

"This might hurt a bit," I said, limply.

We very slowly lifted him, with me holding him under one armpit and the Gurkha under the other. With my other arm I supported his neck, which had only a crude piece of polystyrene to keep it from snapping.

It was like lifting a 90-year-old man out of a wheelchair. His body felt so lifeless, so devoid of strength.

As we moved him, he made tiny pained noises. He sounded like a man at death's door. Whereas Richard yelled and screamed in agony, Hank couldn't even muster the energy to do that.

The blood had started seeping from the bandage at the back of his neck again. I supposed this was from his heart starting to beat very fast with the trauma, and pumping blood out.

When we finally got him to his feet, he was so unsteady, so precariously balanced that he needed constant support, not only due to his injuries, but due to the lack of blood in his system.

"Can you get your cock out?"

"Yeth, yeth," he said.

He could hardly speak because there was so much blood everywhere, all over his face.

He couldn't look down so I held the green bowl up in the air at head height so that he could see it, then lowered it down to his groin.

Without even being able to look down, he managed to fumble and open his flies and do his business. He was more accurate than the Sherpa.

The Gurkha held him while I put the bowl down, and then we lowered him immensely slowly back down again. He continued to make the tiny pained noises that chilled me to my bones.

We then spent ten minutes sliding cushions in here and there underneath him, to try to get him comfortable in the hope that he would get some sleep.

I was completely shattered. My back was killing me, and I was covered in blood and urine. But I knew I would have carried on for another 20 hours if it had been necessary, if I could have helped these people further.

I went back to my book. Finally midnight came. I needed to go and wake John up, so he could take over.

I walked out and the cold hit me like a brick. With the gas heater and the 20 bodies in the tent, it had become very warm inside.

I had also all but forgotten about the destruction outside.

I had walked the trail from the mess tent to my tent countless times over the past few weeks; I knew the route with my eyes closed. John's tent was next to mine.

But the route had completely changed – the avalanche had entirely altered the topography of Base Camp. I staggered about in the darkness, with only my head torch for guidance.

The rocks, tents, landmarks that had paved the way home had all moved – I had no means of navigation.

I fell to my knees in the snow, my head spinning, my body on the brink of exhaustion. I felt like all my systems were shutting down and that I was going to pass out.

That would mean death. Out here, in the open, in the freezing temperatures, I would die.

I didn't come all this way to die.

I forced myself to my feet.

I stumbled to John's tent, fell on my knees and unzipped it.

"John, John, time to get up," I said.

At first, nothing, then...

"Yeah, yeah, no, good, yeah."

I could hear John rustling about in the darkness, then his headlamp torch flicked on. It would take him a while to get his gear on.

"I'll meet you at the hospital mess tent," I said.

I stumbled back the way I had come. This time it was a little easier to remember the path.

About 15 minutes later, John arrived, his bleary eyes looking determined and steadfast. I felt confident in his abilities to take over.

I explained the situation; who had had more painkillers and who had peed. I told him to wake up the Gurkha if he needed any help.

"Go to bed," John said.

I took his advice.

"Night John."

"Night Jules."

It sounded just like it had done all those times in our shared rooms in the lodges on the way up the Khumbu Valley. I instantly thought: "Good night John Boy; Good night Mary Ellen". It's weird how the brain works when it's exhausted.

On the way back to my tent, I stopped to try and wash my hands in the ladies' toilet tent – the men's toilet tent had been destroyed in the avalanche.

There was no water. I pulled out a bottle of hand disinfectant from my pocket and covered my hands in the gel, using the entire bottle. I scrubbed and scraped but I could not remove all of the blood. I could not shift the smell of urine.

I crawled into my tent on all fours – I've never been so tired, so emotionally exhausted. I pulled off my downing jacket and downing trousers and somehow managed to get into the sleeping bag.

I fell into a deep, deep sleep.

In the night, I was awoken by the sound of a scream, a

hysterical scream. I could hear a dreadful wailing in the darkness. I wasn't sure what was going on; I couldn't see a thing.

I managed to unzip my sleeping bag from inside, enough to get my left hand out. I moved my hand around in the darkness, searching for the small pocket on the inside of the tent where I kept my head torch.

I grabbed it, pulled it out and pressed the button on the top to get some illumination.

I sat up, and the dreadful wailing came again. I could see through my tent canvas that the white pod was lit up like a beacon. I realised what the screaming was – it was Katherine from Adventure Consultants, reliving the horrors she had seen the day before.

Her screaming was so eerie – I had never heard anything like it before. I felt desperately sorry for her, and grateful for the fact that I had not had to go through what she had experienced.

I turned off my head torch, shoved it back into the side pocket, lay down flat and closed my eyes.

The day after

The sound of helicopters filled my head.

I opened my eyes, adjusting slowly to the yellow-coloured gloom. For half a second – half a glorious second – I forgot where I was, what I was doing, what had happened.

Then it all came rushing back into my consciousness: Everest Base Camp, the avalanche, the injured people, the stench of blood, sweat and urine, fear. Was it all just a bad dream I'd had? No, that vile smell was still there – that sticky, pungent, bloody, bleachy smell. It seemed to permeate all my clothes. Each and every fibre of material seemed locked in the stench of fear and death. No, it was no dream.

A helicopter passed overhead, casting a shadow on my tent. Helicopters.

My heart lifted slightly – helicopters! We'd been told there would be at least three days of bad weather, three days before any helicopters would be able to reach us.

But here they were – undeniably here.

I wrestled myself free from the clutch of my downing sleeping bag and crawled to the entrance of my tent. I had to see one with my own eyes. I had to be sure I wasn't imagining the sound, that it wasn't some sort of post-traumatic hallucination.

I yanked the zip open and light spilled into the tent. I shielded my eyes and crawled out into the snow.

I could see a helicopter, as cold and real as the snow around my knees. It was coming in to land on the piles of rocks the Sherpas had placed on top of the glacier to act as a helipad.

My heart leapt at the thought that help had arrived. Did this mean that the injured could get real medical help and were going to be transported to hospital – and that it was all over?

I felt a pang of guilt, wishing away the people I had helped keep alive the previous day – wishing away Mark, Richard, the Gurkha captain – but a part of me wanted them to be gone, taken away by a helicopter to become someone else's problem.

Nine hours in that 'hospital' tent had been enough for me. I had steeled myself, prepared myself for another few days of the same, another few days covered in blood and urine, watching people whimpering in agony, with only Paracetamol to give them. It wrenched my very soul and I felt their pain. Too long in that environment would destroy anybody. I wanted the problem to be someone else's responsibility.

As I stood up from my tent and watched the helicopter land, I felt redoubled respect for those in the medical profession.

Few Westerners alive today would have been through what I had been through just eight hours earlier. Only if you were involved in a war zone, or a massive pile-up on the motorway, a tsunami or some other sort of natural disaster, would you be forced to care for so many horrific injuries, tasked with keeping dying people alive for an unknown amount of time.

I'm not sure how I managed it, but I suspected I would return to England a changed man – someone with severe psychological issues – if I had to endure any more time in the hospital tent.

Still...were they actually gone?

A nagging doubt crept into my brain like a snake. What if they were still there – still dying?

I had to find out.

I pulled on my boots and headed to the mess tent, ashamed of myself for praying they'd all been taken away. But I knew that if they were still there, I was going to go straight back into the tent, standing tall. I was going to start looking after them again, and keep looking after them until they were picked up. Somehow I would have to handle it; find the emotional energy from somewhere.

I reached the mess tent, drew a deep breath, and pulled aside the entrance flap.

The stale, dank smell from the night before hit me like a fist. I staggered in, my hand covering my mouth.

It was empty. The tent was completely empty of bodies.

It looked like a recently abandoned medical tent on a battlefield. Bloody rags littered the floor, discarded bedding was strewn about the place. That smell infested everything.

But the bodies were gone...the people were gone.

Mark, Richard, the Gurkha captain and the other 22 injured souls... All of them had been carried off to the helicopters, and flown away down the valley. The problems had been lifted off my shoulders.

I heaved a huge sigh of relief – my duty was officially over.

I heard no news of the injured. We never found out how they got on once they had been airlifted off the mountain. They took off in the helicopters and flew out of my life, just as quickly and suddenly as they had entered it.

I left the tent and found John, who was standing nearby with Louise.

John told me the injured people had been flown out.

"All of them?" I asked.

"Yes," he replied. "The helicopters managed to get in early this morning. They've all gone. First port of call will be the hospital in Lukla, then, presumably, Kathmandu."

Everyone who didn't require urgent medical attention, who was not a priority for the helicopters, had been left at Base Camp.

Of course, there had been a mass exodus on foot during the night. The majority of the Sherpas had left Base Camp to seek news of their families. Many of the climbers had also fled down the valley, in an attempt to get away from the disaster, and probably to try to catch the next flight home, to get out of the country as soon as possible.

That left the rest of us.

I couldn't see the advantage of rushing off to Kathmandu. We were aware by now that the earthquake had struck close to the city; it would be chaos down there. The airports would be choked with people trying to get away.

I was safer here, I decided.

I looked up towards the summit of Everest, hidden behind

the nearer mountains and clouds...

I imagined it stood, much as it had always done, looking proudly over the entire world from its unique vantage point. I was to discover later that the force was so great that Everest had lost a full inch of its height during the earthquake, but this made no difference to the imposing figure that it would cut upon the skyline.

I stumbled into the second mess tent, found a tea bag and a flask of hot water (good old Bill). I made a cup of Her Maj's finest. It tasted so good that it turned the lights back on in my head.

I looked over at John.

"I guess we should clean up the other mess tent," I said.

"I guess."

It was a big job, we had no idea where to start, and we were both exhausted from the exertions of the previous day.

We started by clearing everything out of the mess tent that had served as our hospital ward, pulling out the soiled sleeping bags, mattresses, the chair I'd sat on the previous night, the urine bowl, the bandages, the remnants of the polystyrene we'd used to make the splint for Mark's neck, the blue Paracetamol tablets, the towels, the smelly, wet socks we'd removed from people's soaking feet – they all came out. We aired the sleeping bags and mattresses as best we could, hanging them over rocks in the hope that it would remove some of the smell.

After several hours' work, we had the tent back to something resembling its original state.

We then swept the thin carpet that lay on top of the snow – I could still see the splattering of blood on the carpet from the previous night... As we swept, the sticky, putrid smell came back, along with the stench of old pee.

I opened the back of the tent, to try to get some air passing through it.

We moved the chairs and the long table back inside. We gathered the fake flowers that had adorned the walls before the disaster and put them back up again. This gave the space a touch of normality, returned it to something that resembled a safe place.

A helicopter breezed overhead and landed on the helipad.

"That's come from Camp 1," said John.

We hadn't heard much from Camp 1, but we knew that two expeditions had sent their teams up there just before the earthquake. They had been up there when the earthquake struck.

We knew that there were some 70 people up at Camp 1, and that the earthquake had kicked off an avalanche near them as well. As Camp 1 was positioned in the middle of the flat area at the top of the Ice Fall, with crevasses around it, the force of the avalanche had somehow very narrowly missed the tents on the perimeter of the camp.

Somebody had radioed them to say that the helicopters were focusing on the injured at Base Camp, and that they would be sorted out later...

Once the helicopters had started to fly to Camp 1, they could only take two passengers at a time, as the air was so thin. People were fighting to get onto the helicopters. Panic had clearly set in.

There had also been people up at Camps 2, 3 and 4. We heard later that those at Camps 3 and 4 had been obliged to trek back down to Camp 2, from where they were helicoptered back to Everest Base Camp.

At EBC, 5,400m above sea level, you are higher than any point in Europe, including Mont Blanc, and basically two-thirds of the way up Everest. It is, essentially, a staging area, where climbers acclimatise and wait for their chance to attempt the summit.

On the day of the disaster, Adventure Consultants (AC) had left only a skeleton crew behind at Base Camp. They would soon appreciate how lucky they were to have set off to reach the summit. It was a miracle that Katherine and Angela, who had remained behind, were still alive and unhurt, if emotionally scarred. The three Sherpas had not been so lucky. If the whole AC team had still been at Base Camp when the avalanche hit, the death toll from the avalanche would probably have been doubled.

As the two helicopters descended from Camp 1 to Base Camp, we could see people disembarking from the helicopters in twos, ducking under the whirring propeller blades and heading over to the remnants of their camp.

Someone shouted to the four people from Adventure Consultants who had already managed to get down from Camp 1: "You guys use this tent!" pointing at the old hospital tent we had just about cleared out. I was really glad that we had the other, clean mess tent, but I felt a twinge of guilt – I should be grateful just to be alive, I thought.

It was now lunchtime, and Bill had somehow managed to dish up a good meal – vegetable soup followed by corned beef and beans. It tasted fantastic. I hadn't realised how hungry I was.

We ate in silence, thinking about the predicament of the AC team. In my mind's eye, I could see them picking through the wreckage of their campsite, trying to come to terms with the utter destruction of all their belongings. They were homeless, on a glacial mountainside, miles from anywhere. They had nothing left, nowhere to go. Their mess tents and everything else had been annihilated by the power of the impact.

Not long after, a dishevelled figure approached us, wandering around aimlessly. He was wearing odd shoes; one training shoe and one big, thick summit boot, making him look mildly ridiculous. He wore an expression of confused resignation as he limped around in the snow.

"You've got odd shoes on," I said to him, a bit stupidly.

"These aren't even mine," he replied. "I can't find my shoes."

He tucked his hands under his armpits.

"Come and have a cup of tea," I told him.

We guided him into our tent and set him up with a cup of Her Maj's finest. He clutched it in both hands.

It transpired he was a member of the Adventure Consultants team, who had been up at Camp 1 when the earthquake hit.

"There's nothing left of our campsite," he said. It's incredible. The Sherpas are dead, the tents are destroyed, all of my stuff is gone."

"Are you going to stay here?" I asked.

"Where else can I go? I have nothing – no passport, no plane tickets, no money, no means of communication."

The gravity of his situation struck me. These people were refugees, stuck on a mountain with no way of getting home.

"Stay here, get warm – drink as much tea as you like," I told him.

I ran over to the shelf in the corner.

"Here," I said, as I turned and thrust a packet of ginger nut biscuits into his hands. "Eat some of these. Bill has knocked up some food – you must stay."

The majority of our expedition team was in the mess tent at the time, so we had something of an impromptu meeting.

We decided we'd give up the second mess tent that had served as a hospital tent for the Adventure Consultants team to eat in, and they could use our white pod to sleep in. We could all shuffle up at dinner and fit into one mess tent. At the very least, the two tents would be warm places for them to get their heads down and recoup some energy while they sorted out what they were going to do.

In the end, they spent a couple of days sifting through the wreckage, trying to find lost possessions and save as much as possible of their camp. Then they set off down the mountain, thus restoring to us the use of our tents.

* * * * *

The following day, after a good night's sleep, we moved on to repairing the toilet tent. It had been completely flattened, with the stainless-steel toilet and blue collection barrels blown several metres away, spilling the contents over the ice and rocks. It stank at the best of times, but now...whew!

Still, I preferred it to the smell of the sweat and sickly treacle blood from the other night.

The whole thing was buckled and bent out of shape, but we managed to get it into a condition that vaguely resembled its former self – but a bit shorter. It was usable, at least.

After hours of hard labour, we washed up and packed ourselves into the single mess tent. It was around four o'clock and the sun was setting, taking with it any sense of warmth, to be replaced by the usual chilling cold.

We had all headed quickly to our tents to grab our thick downing jackets and trousers. The Adventure Consultant guys were huddled in the white pod, short of such warm layers – we had put a gas heater in there to help keep them warm, along with sponge mattresses and sleeping bags, but it wasn't really enough.

In our mess tent, everybody was trying to get a seat at the back of the tent, near the gas heater. In the cold, the true horror of the disaster came flooding back.

Luckily, Bill had knocked up some tasty dishes to help keep our minds off it, although anything would probably have tasted great in the circumstances.

As we were about to start eating, the tent flap opened and Lincoln entered, looking flustered. There was no sign of the smile that was usually plastered across his face.

He came straight up to the table.

"I'm going," he said. "I can't be here any more."

We pointed out that it might be worse down the mountain – better the devil you know, and all that, but he was having none of it.

"I've missed too much," he said, his face rigid and assured. "I've missed too much following this stupid dream. If I go now, I might be able to get back for my kid's graduation."

His Texan accent, usually jovial, sounded severe, serious – the sound of a man realising his mistakes.

"I have to go; I'm sorry."

We made no effort to stop him. I thought back to the moment I first met Lincoln, back in the Hyatt Regency in Kathmandu, only a few weeks previously. I thought about how welcoming, cheerful and carefree he was. But a disaster like this has the ability to bring out the true nature in people, and make them see what's truly important. At that point, for Lincoln, it was getting home, getting away from this cursed mountain.

With that, he turned and left. The tent flap closed and he walked out of our lives for good.

Lincoln must have gone to organise a helicopter ride down to Kathmandu. Officially, this shouldn't have been possible, because all the privately owned helicopters that usually serviced climbers in the Khumbu Valley had been recalled by the Nepalese government, and ordered to help in the aid process. But, in practice, here they were, helping out the foreigners on Everest instead of their own people.

It was hard to blame them, and even harder to take a moral stance and not utilise their services. The Nepalese government was extremely poor. It might pay them for their costs, but it just as likely might not. Whereas the Everest expeditions were a much more reliable source of income; they would always pay, because they would be unable to survive on the mountain without helicopter support, and would not want to be blacklisted.

What would you do if you were a pilot in that situation? Would you carry on flying up and down the Khumbu Valley, transporting people around and getting paid for it, or would you go to work in a dangerous area, with about a 50 per cent chance of payment? There was a moral responsibility sure, but Nepal's infrastructure is not sophisticated, and these people need to keep making money to be able to feed their families.

It was a sobering thought, but a harsh reality in a country such as Nepal.

"Maybe he's right," said Paul. "Maybe the expedition's over."

These words rang in my head: 'maybe the expedition's over'. It couldn't be over; it wasn't finished. I hadn't had much of a chance to think it through since the disaster; there'd been too much going on, too much to do. But now that the mountain had returned to its eerie stillness...

It was still there. Everest was still standing. We were still ready, prepared, fully acclimatised. Surely we still had to give it a try. I'd been up this mountain for weeks, sacrificing time I could have spent with my lovely daughters, in order to prepare myself mentally and physically for the challenge that lay ahead. They couldn't just take that away from me.

I knew that if we didn't do it now, I would force myself to come back again – and I really didn't want to go through all this again, to put myself through missing my daughters dreadfully for two months all over again.

Three of the people in our group of ten – nine, now that Lincoln had left – were on their second attempt. Louise and Paul had attempted the summit the year before, but had had their expeditions cancelled due to the Sherpa strike following the deaths of 16 Sherpas in the Icefall. Taka was also trying for the second time.

The Khumbu Icefall, between Base Camp and Camp 1, at 6,200m, is one of the most dangerous parts of the entire ascent. The route through the ever-moving Icefall is littered with crevasses and deadly drops.

Ice doctors are employed by the Nepalese government to plot a safe route through this dangerous terrain each season, laying guide ropes and setting up aluminium ladders, which are lashed together, sometimes four or five at a time, to provide a path across the giant crevasses.

I wondered what condition it was in, whether any of the routes were still navigable, whether any of the crevasse-spanning ladders remained intact. The others were evidently of the same frame of mind.

"The Icefall will be impassable," someone ventured.

"How do you know that?" I said, concerned at the direction the conversation was heading. "We need to go and assess it before making any decision. We know Camp 1 is fine – we've seen the people coming back."

"But they didn't cross the Icefall."

That was true; they were helicoptered back to Base Camp. But that meant nothing until we were able to fully assess the Icefall.

"We need to look, to find out for ourselves, before calling the whole thing off, before giving everything up," I said.

There was silence. I could see they were all torn between their dreams and the reality of the situation.

"Who wants to give up and go home?"

No one raised a hand. No one wanted to give up and go home. Our expedition was still nine strong; nine determined individuals who wanted to reach the top of the world.

I nodded, relieved that I had support, and that I wasn't the only one still wanting to summit.

I left the tent and looked out into the moonlit night across the wreckage of Base Camp. All this devastation, all this loss of life, and still I wanted to get to the top of that bloody mountain. Its draw was irresistible to me... I looked past the abandoned, half-destroyed tents, my eyes meandering slowly up the Khumbu Icefall. I picked out the grey rocks, vivid and contrasting against the brilliant white snow. It was a clear night; not a cloud in the sky. The summit seemed so near, so close, I could almost reach out and grab it. It was mine, that peak; I would make it there.

Was this summit fever?

I'd read about summit fever before, that dangerous state

of mind where even the most experienced of climbers fails to notice adverse weather conditions, impassable mountain routes, even their own physical exhaustion. All they can see is that summit ahead of them. It becomes their entire world – and it consumes them.

Many, many experienced mountaineers have had their lives cut short because of that all-encompassing singular desire to reach their objective. I thought about Green Boots, up there alone on the mountainside, frozen in the same resting place for over a decade.

Green Boots is one of the many bodies climbers pass on their way to the summit – an unknown mountaineer who lost everything in his hunt for glory.

He's called Green Boots because of the luminous coloured boots that he still wears. I'd seen pictures online. It looks as if the guy was just taking a break from his ascent and has fallen asleep. Apart from the layers of snow piling up on him, and his eerie stillness, there is nothing to suggest that he is actually dead. His orange jacket and his blue trousers are still intact; a few empty oxygen cylinders lie discarded next to him.

It looks as if he could get up at any moment, shake the snow off and continue on his way. Unfortunately, he never will. He remains a permanent memorial, a warning sign for would-be climbers. There is no way to remove his body; he was deep in the death zone, helicopters couldn't fly that high and other climbers would die if they attempted something as foolish as carting the body down.

Everest was set to be the unknown man's permanent tomb,

with hundreds of people snapping pictures of his perfectly preserved body on their way to the summit he never reached.

It was a sad sight, but, in a warped kind of way I had been looking forward to seeing him.

He is only one of 200 bodies sharing that gargantuan tomb. They act as landmarks, way points on the route to the top.

The cave in which Green Boots permanently resides was also the final resting place of another – this time in a more controversial situation.

On the way up the Khumbu Valley, I had seen a memorial to a climber who had lost his life while climbing Everest. The valley was littered with memorials and dedication plaques to dead climbers, but I lingered by this one for longer than usual – it was a memorial to an experienced British climber, David Sharp.

In 2006, he attempted to scale Everest for the third time, determined not to be defeated again.

During his ascent, agonisingly close to the top, he ran into difficulties and ran out of energy. Each step must have been like wading through thick treacle; his feet would have felt like lumps of rock holding him down.

He got separated from the others in his group, but he was an experienced climber – they assumed he had bedded down for the night in one of the tents at the higher camps.

In a situation such as this, it is practically impossible to maintain coherent thought. The motivation to keep moving disappears; all you want to do is sit down. And once you do, you've had it. Your body becomes a cumbersome burden, dragging you down into sleep – into death.

Sharp stumbled, blind to logic, and finally stopped at Green Boots' Cave. He collapsed and awaited his fate, knowing full well what he was doing.

That wasn't, however, the end of the story.

Much like the injured man in the story of the Good Samaritan, dozens of climbers passed Sharp without stopping, without assisting him. Some tried, but were unable to help – there was nothing that could be done. To stop would have put them at risk of suffering the same fate. At the very least, it would have destroyed any chance they had of reaching the summit.

They all had limited oxygen in their tanks, and did not have the energy to lift or help this half-frozen man. They had to leave him to die.

It was suggested that many of the climbers who passed David Sharp mistook him for Green Boots and continued on their way. Sharp would have been too physically exhausted to cry out, to get their attention. He would have watched them through frozen eyes, knowing full well that they were his only chance of survival, yet powerless to stop them from continuing on their way and disappearing into the distance.

Mark Inglis was among those who passed David Sharp as he lay dying that day.

Inglis, a climber from New Zealand, was attempting to become the first double-amputee to reach the summit of the mountain.

They arrived at Green Boots' Cave – 8,412 metres above sea level – at about one in the morning, coming across the huddled body of Sharp not far from Green Boots himself.

They unclipped their ropes, passed Sharp and clipped back on again. They believed him to be in a hypothermic coma – they believed he was essentially already dead.

Sharp's eyes were frozen shut; his nose was turning a gruesome black with frostbite. There was very little chance that Inglis and his team could have done anything to help him. But Inglis was to receive a lot of criticism for his decision to carry on. In fact, whether he was aware of what he was doing or not – whether he knew that he was leaving a man to die so that he himself could stand on top of the world for a few precious minutes – was something very few people could ever really know or fully appreciate.

David Sharp died on Everest that day, another skilled, successful climber to succumb to the brutality of the mountain.

Summit fever is a very real thing; it is a dangerous, potent killer, as deadly as the snow, the frostbite, the falling rocks. Diagnosing it is difficult, but rationalising with those suffering from it is almost impossible.

I asked myself again, was *I* suffering from summit fever? Was the lure of the mountain clouding my judgment?

No, this wasn't the same. The opportunities were still there – we had all the kit required, the correct support, a willing team and clement weather. We weren't mountain-crazy; we were making a logical, informed decision based on the evidence available to us.

The next morning, I decided to have a recce of EBC, to see how bad things were further afield. I had only seen the area immediately surrounding our camp. I'd had too much to do in our makeshift hospital tent to allow me to wander around EBC. I wanted to see how everything was, because this place was still going to be our home for the foreseeable future.

I grabbed my camera from my tent and headed out.

As I made my way through Base Camp, the true extent of the devastation became clear. The closer I drew to the area hit hardest by the avalanche, the fewer upright tents remained. Those still standing were the lucky ones that had been positioned behind immovable rocks or outcrops.

Even some of the larger rocks – weighing several tons – had moved. They'd been picked up and thrown through the air.

The glacier on which EBC was positioned was carrying some enormous boulders down the mountainside. So when the avalanche hit, many of these flew around, and if you were in the way...

At the time of the avalanche, there were three men sitting chatting in one tent. One of these large rocks was picked up by the avalanche and blasted through the tent, straight through the guy in the middle. The other two were fine, but the one in the middle was killed outright. If the rock had gone just 30 centimetres either side of its actual course, one of the other two men would have been its victim instead.

I thought again how lucky I was to be alive It was pure luck which of us lived and which of us died: Russian roulette.

As I moved towards the Adventure Consultants camp, where the avalanche had hit the hardest, it looked more and more like a war zone. Tents lay flattened, with huge rocks over them, tent poles protruded like broken limbs. Miscellaneous items were scattered everywhere. I had to watch my step to avoid tripping over lost clothing and hiking equipment.

It was a looter's paradise. There was expensive, specialised equipment everywhere; high-quality branded goods littered the floor – laptops, Kindles, solar panels, phones... It was like a patchwork quilt of overlapping experiences, a muddled mess of the lives of those caught up in that brutal moment.

I picked up a laptop, brushed off the snow and placed it on a rock. If the owner came back, he or she might have a better chance of finding it.

The Adventure Consultants camp itself was just a desolate area, covered in snow. There was one person wandering aimlessly around, digging here and there in the snow.

A red mess tent, with 'Adventure Consultants' printed on it in large letters, was a crumpled, smashed-up heap. How Angela and Katherine had managed to get out of it alive was anyone's guess.

A huge rock, large enough to completely cover an entire tent, sat proudly in the centre of the campsite, having been carried and dumped there by the avalanche.

How lucky the majority of the team was to have been up at Camp 1. If they'd been here, they would be dead. Simple as that. Very few of them would have survived. I heard that one man had been blown 250 metres out of his tent, and smashed to pieces in the Icefall.

Even as it was, what a shock the AC group must have had, returning to EBC to find nothing left.

I started to dig around, pulling up ripped canvas, lost hiking boots, a huge array of personal belongings. Every time I thrust my glove-clad hand into the snow to pull something out, I had no idea what I would find... I feared pulling my hand out of the snow gripping another, colder, dead hand – that I would have to dig up the frozen corpse of someone just like me, a person who had wanted to achieve his or her lifelong dream...but had died in the process.

I kept digging – I didn't find any bodies.

How many were there, though, underneath our feet? How many people hadn't been found? How many had been tossed hundreds of metres from Base Camp, smashed to pieces in quiet, secluded areas?

Base Camp was a chaotic mess of a place, but the shouting, running and screaming of the previous day had been replaced by an eerie stillness, an odd silence. The few people who remained blundered around, dazed and confused, like zombies with no purpose.

No one really knew what to do, but we were trying to get our lives back on track as best we could.

I got my camera out. People had to see this; they had to understand what had happened, the level of the devastation up on Everest.

I started snapping some pictures of some of the affected areas. I felt guilty about it, but I wanted to be able to explain to people afterwards what it was like. Sometimes words aren't good enough.

"It's not a fucking tourist attraction," came a voice from

behind a rock.

I turned to face its owner; he looked up challengingly, his face set and serious.

"I know," I said. "I just want to capture what it's like here."

"Fuck off and do it somewhere else."

I think he must have been one of the camp business owners, and he sounded very angry, so I decided it was time to leave.

Elia, Donald's photographer, had had a similar experience when trying to document the carnage. He had been trying to take some photographs and carry out some interviews. CNN had contacted him via his Sat-Phone and were very interested to get firsthand accounts. He had approached the wrong man, at the wrong time. He was reassuringly told that if he took another photograph, he would have his "fucking face smashed in".

The tension in the air at Base Camp was now palpable. There was a lot of anger, resentment and silent rage, particularly from those who ran the expeditions. This was their livelihood. They hadn't just lost an expensive downing jacket or a pair of summit boots; they'd lost their entire business and livelihood. I later found out that one of the expedition leaders had also lost his house in Kathmandu.

Many of the expeditions struggle to get insurance for the expensive equipment necessary to reach the summit, because of the very high risk of damage or destruction. They take a risk, purchasing the equipment in the hope that nothing major will happen, and that they can make back the money from the expedition members of film crews.

But now, something major *had* happened, and these people had just lost hundreds of thousands of pounds' worth of specialist equipment.

They would also still have to cart all their wrecked equipment back down the mountain. The Nepalese government has a policy in which everything is weighed before being allowed up to EBC, and a deposit paid, then it is all weighed again on the way back down, in order to ensure that no rubbish is left behind at the end of the season. In a normal situation, this is a great initiative, intended to prevent EBC from becoming a rubbish tip again, as it had been in the old days, littered with discarded tents, oxygen bottles, food waste, etc. But I felt sorry for the expedition companies having to trawl through the desolation to find all their belongings.

I left AC's camp. I felt I had overstayed my welcome.

I walked back past the crude, improvised helipad – helicopters continued to zigzag overhead. Next to the stones that made up the landing area, there was a line of blue tarpaulin and tied-up canvas tents. At first, I couldn't quite figure out what they were, these bundles of haphazardly tied material, sitting next to the helipad.

A helicopter flew close overhead, whipping up a gale as it came in to land.

The tarpaulin nearest to me flapped in the wind, uncovering the horror that was hidden inside. I jumped back in shock.

The pale, ghostly body of a man lay unmoving inside, his half-frozen hair ruffled by the draught from the helicopter. I stopped walking, stunned by the sudden realisation of what was in those packages.

Two days ago, this man was just like me – here for the expedition of a lifetime. But now he was wrapped in a broken piece of tarpaulin, his eyes frozen closed forever. And here I was, standing next to him, unscathed, unhurt. Why him and not me? I saw our roles reversed, pictured myself in his canvas grave, as he stood above me looking down at my lifeless body...

Two men picked up the corpse, carried it up into the helicopter and loaded it in. They ducked away from the blades as it took off.

I watched the helicopter rise into the air, dip its nose and head in the direction of Kathmandu. The body in the tarpaulin was being carried off to his loved ones wherever his home was. Others remained, wrapped up on the floor near the helipad, quietly waiting in line for their lifts.

I made my way back to my camp, trying my best to shake off what I had seen, and remain positive. A positive attitude was key. If I didn't maintain a positive outlook, I knew I'd be scrambling to get on the next helicopter out of here.

It was a harsh reality, but we were all just trying to get on with our lives. The reality was we still had a job to do to survive in that desolate environment, so it was not helpful to dwell on what we couldn't change.

I wanted desperately to contact my family again – my girls, dad, brother and Vicky – to let them know how I was getting on. I had managed to talk to them briefly on the Sat-Phone the night before, but it wasn't really enough.

The only way to get any sort of communication out without

a Sat-Phone was to trek down to Gorak Shep, but the chaos down the Khumbu Valley basically ruled that out as an option at this point.

We'd heard that a lot of the villages in the Khumbu Valley – Pheriche, Namche Bazaar, Gorak Shep – had all been destroyed, the poorly constructed buildings collapsing under the pressures of the earthquake.

Even if I managed to get down the valley, where was I going to go? What was I going to do? It was better to stay put, and wait for normality to return. We had eight weeks' worth of food and infinite amounts of fresh water from the snow, we were in good shape – the best thing to do was to stay at EBC.

That evening, Bill knocked up a meal, and we all squeezed into the one mess tent to eat. It was a surreal occasion – all of us eating as if nothing had changed. We were all wedged in next to each other, all wearing our thick downing jackets to keep us warm.

Angelica, our doctor, announced to us that she had got engaged just before the disaster. Her boyfriend was also camped at Base Camp, working and living with another expedition.

He had found a plastic ring on the way up the Khumbu Valley and had hatched a plan to propose to her at Base Camp. In light of the avalanche, they'd decided to delay the announcement until everything had calmed down a little. The whole thing can't have felt like a particularly good omen for them.

But naturally, we decided to celebrate, so we made a

table for them to eat at – silver service at 5,400m. We used pillowcases to make posh napkins and put some plastic flowers in a jar in front of them. It was the best we could do, given the situation, but it made the moment feel more special, and it also gave us something to focus on, to take our minds off the events of the last 36 hours.

We put some of the silk well-wishing scarves around their necks – it seemed appropriate to use this local good-luck custom.

It was an odd occasion – so much cheerful conversation and well-wishing for these two as they embarked on their lives together, when we'd just experienced how easily lives could be ripped apart in the blink of an eye. Twenty-four hours earlier, we'd all been in hell on earth, and now, here we were, singing, cheering and clapping, celebrating this lovely moment. It felt surreal. Deep sorrow and deep happiness were all mixed up together.

We had no idea how the expedition was going to turn out, whether we were going to be able to attempt the summit, but life went on as best it could at Everest Base Camp.

Life goes on – but the expedition?

It had been a couple of days now since the earthquake, and although our surroundings still resembled something from a war zone, an element of normality had returned.

People were going about their business, getting stuff done – tents were being repaired, lost items were being collected, thoughts were beginning to turn back to Everest.

Over the past few days, we'd all seen tragedies few contemporary Westerners can claim to have seen. Each one of us would be affected differently. Some would never get over the shock of what they'd seen.

I thought of Katherine, waking in the white pod each night, screaming uncontrollably.

I thought of Lincoln, packing his bags and abandoning ship, his face ashen, all the humour in this big, cuddly Texan's eyes extinguished.

I wondered how all this was going to affect me. Would I

suffer from some sort of post-traumatic stress? My brain had a good way of rationalising things that happened, but had this perhaps pushed my brain too far? Was it going to scramble my wires? Was my mind tough enough to cope?

People react to events in different ways, and here at Base Camp there was a wide range of emotional reactions. Some people couldn't cope, and were drinking heavily every afternoon, others had outbursts of great rage and anger, some smoked lots of joints (goodness knows where the stuff comes from – climbers always seem to have a stash). And some kept quiet, bottling up their feelings.

My grandfather was a butcher, and when I was a kid, my brother and I used to watch him kill cows and sheep in his abattoir. The sheep would be put in a cradle, and he would stun them before slitting their throats to bleed them quickly. This made the meat more tender. With the cattle, he would herd them one by one into a pen, poke their heads through a slot with a metal bar that kept them still. He would shoot a bolt straight into their brains to kill them and then remove the pen. The cow would slump over onto its side and my grandfather would then slit them up the middle, right there and then on the floor. He'd remove all the organs while they were still hot and steamy.

I was three years old when he first took me up to the abattoir to watch the slaughter. We'd watch him cut out the heart, the liver, the lungs, the intestines, everything. We'd watch him hang them all on S-shaped hooks and then hang the hooks on the metal rails that ran around the wall of the slaughter shed.

We used to grab the butcher's steel, a knife-sharpening rod with a handle, and whack the hearts. They were so fresh, the nerve endings would twitch and the heart would make a quiet buzzing sound. It was as if the heart were still alive, and we found it fascinating.

"Go on Rick, hit it again."

"It's your turn Ju. Whack it, whack it harder."

To us, it was just part of our family business, and we thought it quite normal.

The amount of blood that poured out of the sheep was incredible. Blood would come pumping out, gushing out; it was extraordinary.

After he was done, my grandfather would shout to us, "Go on lads, get the buckets. Wash the blood down."

We'd be running around – aged three, four or five – filling buckets with water from the sink and swilling down the yard, washing away the blood. And it was great fun; we laughed the whole time. It was just how things were done, how they had been done for hundreds of years. It was a way of life that I had become used to at a very young age.

Perhaps that's why I hadn't broken down, why I was able to hold it all together so far. I'd seen things I'd never forget, things I wouldn't wish on my worst enemy, but perhaps I was able to dissociate myself from the smell of the blood, the pain, the destruction in a way that others would struggle to do.

I wasn't sure if that was a good thing or not...

At night, Base Camp was now eerily silent, punctuated only by the howling wind and the petrified screams of Katherine, the physio. As I walked back to my tent in the darkness, the only thing I could see was the orange glow of a head torch, from somebody unable to sleep, reading a book. Everything else was pure blackness, my path lit only by the light of my head torch. I found myself wondering about the spirits of those who had died.

Were they floating about us now?

The hair on the back of my neck prickled. I'm not superstitious, but I wondered about these spirits – whether they would have gone by now, or whether they would still be floating around Base Camp with unfinished business, wondering why they had been chosen and not us. It really was like a lottery.

The official number of dead at that time was 19, though some people had not been accounted for. That figure would rise to 22 as time went by and more bodies were found under the debris.

* * * * *

The next day, I decided to go to check out the Icefall for myself. I'd heard rumours that it was impassable, unclimbable, and that there was no hope for anyone attempting to summit this year. It had been stated that the ladders that spanned the crevasses throughout the Icefall had apparently all collapsed. But how did anybody know? No one had tried to climb it.

I wanted to have a look at it, to see what condition it was really in. I doubted anyone had actually tried to climb it; most people seemed to be content to believe the products of the rumour mill, which was now in overdrive.

I had no idea at this point whether we were going to carry on, or if the expedition would be called off. At least, I thought, we could have all the facts before making a decision.

More and more expeditions were leaving. Our hopes of summiting were dribbling away with them, as we needed a fair bit of Sherpa manpower to get the ropes in place, which meant a combined effort by the Sherpas from several expeditions.

To reach the base of the Khumbu Icefall, I walked through Base Camp and then headed up through the forest of jagged ice pillars to the bottom of the Fall. These pillars of ice were between 20 and 30 metres high, creating a labyrinth in which it would be very easy to get lost.

After the earthquake, many pillars had become unstable; some had collapsed altogether. I walked through slowly, carefully, always on the alert for the jarring sound of breaking ice. The sound of the snow crunching under my feet echoed through the near-silence.

As the warm midday sun beat down, I could see the ice melting, drips of water running down the side of the glistening ice pillars. Maybe I'd chosen a foolish time to go wandering off on my own... Oh well, too late now. I pressed on.

Soon, and with no small amount of relief, I arrived at the blue tent at the bottom of the Icefall. SPCC – Sagarmatha Pollution Control Committee – was printed on the side in large, white lettering. This tent was essentially border control for the mountain, where government officials checked the permits of everyone attempting to climb.

In the recorded history of Everest, only one person has managed to sneak past and climb the mountain without the proper paperwork. The officials run a pretty tight ship, as Everest alone generates a third of the government's tourist income each year. Yes I did say that, a *third*!

Of course, the tent was empty. The SPCC team had all gone down the mountain immediately after the earthquake hit, to check on their families. All other governmental officials had also disappeared pretty quickly.

Near the tent, I saw something glistening in the sunshine. I walked over to it.

At first, I couldn't figure out what it was. A large, metallic object, twisted and buckled into a peculiar shape.

When Bill boiled water for tea, he would store it in large tea urns. These were heavy-duty containers, built out of double-walled stainless steel to keep them insulated.

This was the wrecked remains of a huge tea urn. It had been thrown at least 300 metres from Base Camp by the force of the avalanche, and had almost smashed to pieces on impact. If anybody had been unlucky enough to find themselves in that tea urn's path, it would have been certain death.

A pair of salopettes lay neatly near the tea urn, as if somebody had decided to take them off, put them down carefully and then run on up the Icefall. They looked so out of place there, hundreds of metres away from any of the tents in Base Camp. I left them where they lay.

As I stood at the bottom of the Khumbu Icefall, the first real step of the mountain on the route to the summit, I realised how much I wanted to get up there.

I knew that I shouldn't, that no one would think less of me if I turned around, packed up my belongings and left Everest Base Camp for good. But I also knew I couldn't live with myself if I didn't do everything in my power to have a crack at the top.

I'd survived the earthquake, the avalanche; I'd hopefully helped save some lives. I was here, I was alive, I had suffered -15°C for many nights, I was acclimatised, I had taken two months out – and I still wanted to try for the summit. I did not want to have to come back again.

I knew it would be difficult to explain to those who had never stood at the bottom of the Khumbu Icefall. They would struggle to understand my reasoning, my rationale. But it was clear to me. I just knew I had to give my all to get up that mountain. I didn't want to have to spend weeks getting to Base Camp and acclimatising all over again. I was ready and willing, I wanted to get up that mountain, get it over and done with...

I walked back from the Icefall in a bit of a daze, navigating the potentially treacherous forest of ice towers with only faint interest.

As I followed the stream that flowed along the path of the glacier, and came within sight of Base Camp; the now-familiar sight of destroyed tents flapping in the wind greeted me.

I spent the rest of the day keeping myself mostly to myself. I felt that the expedition was in jeopardy, but no one was really talking about it. Here we were, at Everest Base Camp, with no one wanting to talk about Everest. Yet the mountain still towered over us all day, a colossal elephant in the living room.

Bill excelled himself with dinner. He'd somehow managed to get some frozen duck, which he cooked with *dauphinoise* potatoes, sautéed carrots and a *hoi sin* sauce. I talk a lot about mealtimes but these really were the peak of each day, when everyone came together to talk. Other than this, unless it was a climbing day, there was really absolutely nothing to do.

We crammed into the mess tent and tucked in. It felt bizarre; there we were, eating duck and *dauphinoise* potatoes, when 22 people had just died and over 100 had been injured, in the very place where we were dining.

Everybody just got on with it – we were either going to laugh or cry.

As I ate, unusually quiet, I thought about Mark. I thought about the 12 hours that I nursed him, kept him alive, comforted him and told him he was going to be all right. The reality was that I had no idea if he was going to be all right. I now had no idea if he was even still alive.

He had been helicoptered off with the rest of the seriously injured, down to Lukla, and then presumably to Kathmandu. The hospitals there weren't exactly world-class at the best of times, but after an earthquake of that magnitude...

Someone squeezed into the space next to me on the bench. *Hoi sin* sauce spilled onto the table as he dumped his plate down.

"Huw's it?" said a gruff voice.

I looked up into the bright eyes of Iwan.

"The Icefall," he continued, his Polish accent somehow

more pronounced. "Can ve go?"

"It didn't look that bad," I said. "But I only went to the bottom; I didn't go up."

"Ve go then," he said simply. "Have proper look."

He seemed deadly serious, as he tucked into his duck.

"OK then," I replied.

"Tumorrow. Early – before sunrise."

Iwan looked up from his dinner just long enough for me to catch a wry smile on his face.

I spent the evening in the white pod with Iwan, discussing the plan for the following morning. Eventually, the guides started to realise what we were planning, and the rumour spread around our expedition group like wildfire.

I could see the irritation in some of the guides' eyes. I couldn't really understand why – we were here to climb a mountain. That was what we had come all this way to do, what we'd all paid through the nose for, so why were we all now just sitting around, waiting, not even trying to find out if our objective was still achievable?

The guides kept telling us that the Icefall was impassable, that the force of the earthquake had destroyed all the aluminium ladders that crossed the deep crevasses, that the ice had shifted and that there was no way through.

They might be right, but they had no way of knowing for sure without someone going to take a look. I had been to the base of the Icefall, and it didn't seem too bad to me.

Sure, the earthquake may have dislodged ice and opened crevasses, but it could just as easily have shaken all the loose ice off the mountain, making the route safer. Someone needed to go up and have a look. Boots on the ground, to coin a management/army phrase.

The Khumbu Icefall is never safe – it is the single most dangerous section on the route to the summit. If you're climbing up it and a large piece of ice – some are the size of skyscrapers – dislodges at that very moment and comes down, the chances are, you are pretty much toast. This is how, very sadly, 16 Sherpas had died the previous year.

So everybody goes up at night or in the early morning, before the sun comes up and starts to melt the ice.

Everything we did at Base Camp was a risk; the whole expedition was a calculated risk, but the adrenalin and sense of achievement was why we did it, why we huddled into a freezing tent, drawing thin air into our lungs, 5,400m above sea level.

Iwan and I even offered to go and survey the route to Camp 1 for the guides, but that only seemed to aggravate them further. Actually, many of them had already left EBC in spirit; I'd overheard them openly discussing holiday plans. While they sat in their downing jackets, crammed into the mess tent like the rest of us, they were dreaming about chilling out in Thailand on the beach with a hot Thai girl for the remaining three weeks of their assignment.

In the cold light of day, they had no real incentive to push on. They would get paid for the full two months, even though we'd only been there for five weeks.

Most expedition companies are run by climbers, who are

not natural business people, so their business model is not a good one – especially for such a high-risk business. You want your staff incentives to help your "clients" achieve their goals. If you tell your staff they will receive full pay even if they didn't achieve the clients' goals, there is no incentive for the guides and Sherpas employed to help us get to the top of the mountain – to carry on past halfway.

You should incentivise them at each step of the way. For example, give them a bonus for getting EBC set up and getting everybody safely to EBC, then another bonus for Camp 1, Camp 2 etc. It could be argued that this encourages them to take unnecessary risks, but Everest is, by its nature, a very risky operation. At least this way, the guides and Sherpas are incentivised to achieve the overall goal.

Iwan and I had far from given up, and we continued to plan. If we could prove the Icefall was passable, and that Camp 1 was still in a reasonable condition, we would be in a much stronger position to persuade the expedition to continue.

As we sat in the corner, discussing our "treasonous" plot, we were approached by a couple of people I hadn't seen before. They spoke in Polish to Iwan.

Iwan introduced me and we shook hands. They were a Polish father and son, Petar and Andrzej, whose dream had been to climb Everest together, but who did not possess the funds to join one of the Western expeditions. They had paid just to have a tent pitched with one of the cheap Nepalese expeditions at BC. They had no guides and no Sherpas. The father was in his 60s, the son around 45. And they'd already heard about our plan.

They had already taken a lot of their own expensive equipment up to Camp 1 in preparation for their summit attempt. Of course, the earthquake and avalanche had hit, and Camp 1 had been abandoned.

They'd been down at Base Camp at the time, so their equipment had been stranded at Camp 1.

Andrzej spoke to us in English.

"You go?"

"Maybe," said Iwan.

Petar said something in Polish to his son, looking at him angrily. Andrzej snapped back.

"He does not vant him to go," Iwan translated for me. "Thinks too dangerous."

I felt terribly sorry for the pair of them. Iwan told me they could not afford to pay a helicopter to fly up to Camp 1 to pick up their equipment, and Petar felt it was very risky to climb up to Camp 1 to get it. He told Iwan his wife would never forgive him if anything happened to his son.

It was very dark now, and the tent was clearing as people made their way to bed. I decided to let Iwan continue his conversation with his compatriots, and said my goodnights.

"Six am," whispered Iwan as I got up to leave.

I nodded, filled my Nalgene bottle with warm water, zipped up my downing jacket, pulled my beanie hat down over my head, turned on my head torch and stepped out into the freezing darkness.

Up the Icefall
with rising hopes

My watch alarm went off at 5am.

I groaned in the darkness, I was very, very tired, extremely cold (-15°C really is cold), and I was unsure if this was really a good idea. But I'd agreed to go, and actually felt quite honoured that Iwan thought me a worthy climbing companion. I was not going to let him down, and my rucksack was packed ready.

I pulled on my climbing trousers over the underwear and socks that I had not changed for five days. I put on another pair of thick climbing socks, pulled on my downing jacket and moved to the outer patio area. I laced up my Everest boots, all three layers, with great difficulty.

I was cold, tired, hungry and...actually, quite scared.

I climbed out into the darkness and looked around. It was pitch black, and my head torch picked out the little orange blobs of the tents littered around the glacier. I swung my rucksack on to my back, grabbed my ice axe and headed to the mess tent. I needed some sugar energy.

I peered inside – Iwan was already there.

"Morning."

"Hey Jules! Gut morning!"

He was far too cheerful for this time of morning.

"Are yu ridy?"

"Er, yeah... I guess so." I was far from sure.

The Icefall was the most dangerous part of Everest, nobody knew what condition it was in. This could well be my last day on earth, I thought.

It was very dark outside, but Iwan had switched on the solar bulb in the mess tent and there was just enough energy in the battery from yesterday for us to see to eat.

I grabbed a bowl and three Weetabix, pouring a pile of sugar and powdered milk on top. I pulled over one of the large hot water flasks and filled the bowl, mushing the whole lot up. It was like a bowl of very warm sugary porridge, and as I huddled there, cold and tired in the poor light, to me, it tasted fantastic.

I grabbed a mug and made myself a cup of Her Maj's finest, lukewarm tea.

All this in the space of five minutes, as we had to get to the bottom of the Icefall for six to give us a good, clear two hours of climbing, and enough time to get back down before the sun came up and started melting the bloody thing.

Iwan looked over at me.

"Yu ridy?"

"As I'll ever be.

We grabbed our rucksacks and ice axes, and headed out into the eerie darkness.

Iwan told me he had been to see Donald the night before, to tell him of our intention to climb the Icefall, and to clear it with him. Iwan was part of Donald's team; he had been employed as a professional guide to assist Donald in his 8,000m peak charity challenge. Donald was OK about Iwan going, but told him to be extra careful – any injuries could result in bad publicity for his charity.

It was a cold, misty morning. The light from our head torches bounced along in front of us as we made our way down to the stream that ran alongside Base Camp, over the glacier. We crossed the stream and trekked alongside it for some 20 minutes, heading towards the base of the Icefall. We then ducked in among the eerie giant serac pillars, which towered some 30 metres above us, looking for the little red flags that showed the way to the official start of the Icefall and the rope the Icefall doctors had installed some weeks earlier. If you couldn't find the start of the rope, you had no chance. In the earthquake, some of the flags had been blown away, so it was no mean feat just finding the base of the Icefall in among those ghostly pillars – they seemed almost to creep around in the dark.

I felt a shiver run down my spine.

We walked in silence, the crunch of the snow under our feet was deafening. Navigating around these huge structures was very difficult.

I breathed heavily. It was exhausting work, trucking through the fresh snow, trying to force a path. I could see my breath streaming out in front of me in the cold light of my head torch.

Iwan stopped suddenly. I did the same.

"What?" I whispered.

Iwan crouched down in the snow.

"Footprints."

I looked down at the snow where he was crouched. He was right. There was a single set of footprints heading in the same direction as we were.

I thought about the yeti skull at Khumjong.

Casting my light forward, I saw the footprints continue towards the Khumbu Icefall.

"Ve follow," said Iwan.

They were probably my footprints from the day before. I couldn't be sure; I had no idea what route I had taken through the seracs.

Hold on, that didn't seem right – they were fresh tracks – and it had snowed last night, so if they were mine they would be covered in fresh snow by now.

Whose were these then? Who could be foolish enough to take this route, at night, alone?

The wind continued howling through the giant ice pillars, dashing loose snow into our faces. I was very glad I was not alone. Even with my Polish friend, it was very eerie, and we were miles from any help.

We followed the footprints to the bottom of the Icefall, where we kneeled to put on our crampons.

Iwan broke the silence.

"After avalanche," he said, "we found body over there."

He pointed off in the distance. I looked, as if I would be able to see something.

"We – me and Donat – were telling people to go. Donat

moved a tent and an arm [Iwan grabbed his right forearm with his left] was out of the snow. We dug him up. Frozen solid, blood everywhere."

"Jeepers."

The area where Iwan was pointing was a full 250 metres from Base Camp. This poor man would have been flung from Base Camp by the force of the avalanche, all the way over to the seracs.

"His teeth, his mouth, gone. His ears touching his nose. His legs wrapped around his head."

Iwan put his hands inside his mouth and yanked them back hard, pulling his mouth wide open to demonstrate what the face looked like. I felt a shiver run down my spine again.

A grotesque image formed in my mind. Pure white snow splattered with blood.

"We tried to straighten out body...too cold. We wrapped in plastic, and he was taken away."

Iwan's face was wrapped up tightly now. Only his eyes were showing – two tiny windows into the soul. His stare bored into the distance.

There was silence for a time. Everybody at Base Camp that day had seen atrocities. We would all keep those vivid, lurid images until the day we died.

We were now at the SPCC tent. Iwan grabbed a bit of rope from a coil that lay next to the tent, cut some off and used it to tie us together. There was about 10 metres of rope between us.

Without another word, he turned and began climbing the

Icefall. Without a word, I followed, my crampons crunching in the snow and my ice axe gripped tightly in my right hand.

This was the first time I had set foot into the heart of the Khumbu Icefall. I was nervous – I'd heard so many rumours about how terrible and dire it was, how it was hell on earth, how you could hear the sound of seracs cracking and falling all around you. Here we were, climbing a route that everybody had said was impassable, and without any support...without knowing what dangers lay ahead.

The rope that the ice doctors had laid through the Icefall was usable in places, and we clipped in with our jumars. Strictly speaking, you shouldn't use the rope to haul yourself up, but everybody does, and by now I was gasping for air. It was one step and four breaths, one step, four breaths. We hiked on upwards, sticking our crampons into the thick snow in front of us.

Because of the earthquake and avalanche, the whole thing seemed quite unstable. The rope at the side was quite slack; not much good at all. If a crevasse opened up beneath us and we fell connected to slack rope, we were going to fall quite some distance before it tightened up and arrested us – if it did at all before we hit the bottom...

Still, it felt better to be clipped on to something than nothing.

After about 20 minutes navigating the large lumps of ice and boulders, panting like mad the entire time, we arrived at the first aluminium ladder.

We were aware that there were some four sets of ladders to cross to get to an area called the "football pitch". This area was not far from Camp 1, and was an unofficial resting place, as it was relatively flat and open, and hence relatively – and I say 'relatively' in Everest terms – safe. The ladders are used to cross the crevasses. These ladders were the main reason we were told that the route was impassable – it was understood that they had all collapsed.

I was stunned; contrary to the rumour mill, the aluminium ladder – a little crooked, perhaps – continued to span the gap, along with the slack rope running next to it.

"Are you going first Iwan?"

"*Tak*," he said, nodding.

I was very glad. Nothing seemed to spook this tough Polish climber, and if truth be known, I was a bit chuffed that he deemed me a suitable climbing partner.

I followed Iwan when he had successfully made it to the other side.

This was a double ladder, with the two ends overlapping by a couple of rungs and lashed together with a bit of climbing rope. There was no way I would do this at my farm and climb up it, but it was considered normal here, and there was no other way of spanning the crevasses. We just got on with it.

Moving with crampons is not easy, but walking over an aluminium ladder in crampons, with a 30-metre drop below? Bloody impossible. Luckily, my feet are of a decent size, so I was able to span two rungs with one step, with my back spikes hanging over the last rung and my front ones hanging over the front.

The ladder creaked as I crossed, the rope lashings in the

middle tightening with my added 90 kilos. If it buckled, that was it; I would be sent plummeting into the abyss below, praying that the slack rope that I was clipped into would go tight before I hit the bottom.

If we both fell and the rope didn't hold us, and we somehow managed to survive the drop, we'd be stuck at the bottom of the crevasse. No one would know where we were, and nobody would come to rescue us. We would die down there, slowly freezing to death.

I focused on each individual step, locking my crampon into the next rung ahead and trying to balance on these two very wobbly ladders.

At last, I took the final step off the ladder, on to the snow at the far side. I fell to my knees, exhausted, and breathed a huge sigh of relief. This was followed by five very quick breaths as I tried to get my breath back. I was exhausted.

Iwan patted me on the back. I dragged myself to my feet and we continued.

In places, the rope was buried under large lumps of ice, so we had to unclip, navigate the obstacle unaided, and then clip back in.

In spite of the fact that I could not get enough air in my lungs, I started to enjoy myself. I was really excited, now that Iwan and I were actually climbing Everest.

This was why I'd come to Everest in the first place. Doing Base Camp was fun, but this was the real deal – the adrenalin pumping, the sense of excitement and achievement. I'd felt a little lost at Base Camp, worried that the expedition wasn't going to go any further. But here I was, climbing Everest – without any Sherpa support! It was a truly exhilarating feeling.

It was getting lighter by this point; we could actually see the route and a little of the view. I could just make out the white peak of Pulmori across the valley.

We came up to the second ladder. It had been set to enable us to climb a large snow step some five metres high, and it had managed to survive the earthquake intact. We clipped into the slack rope next to it and climbed it easily.

Our mood began to rise. The climb was hard, gruelling work, but it was clear that we were both in our element.

As we approached the third intact ladder, I saw them again. The footprints.

"Iwan, it's those footprints again."

He nodded.

"Someone has been up here – the rope has been pulled from the snow."

That was true. Apart from the impassable parts of the route up the Icefall, the rope had been pulled out of the fresh snow. Somebody had already been up the Icefall ahead of us – but who? The ghost of a dead person? The thought made my spine tingle.

We carried on, soon arriving at a section where the ice had collapsed over the route and we had to find a way to climb up and over a huge ice boulder. This meant walking along a very small ledge on the boulder, some 10 metres above the snow below, and then scrambling up on top of it.

Iwan clipped into the slack rope and pulled it tight.

"*Tak*, OK!".

He grabbed his ice axe in his right hand and started to shuffle along the ledge, stabbing the axe into the snow above his head as he went. He got to the edge of the ledge and then had to pull himself on to the top of the massive boulder.

He threw his axe hard, high above him, and then slid the jumar up and pulled hard on both. If the rope was loose above him, or if it snapped, he would have to rely completely on the ice axe or he would fall...

He pulled hard and with one very swift and professional move, he disappeared out of sight on to the top of the boulder.

"Now yu!"

Jeepers. Was this really such a good idea, and should we carry on? I was rasping on the thin air and I had extreme doubts at this point. I could feel my sphincter twitching hard, but I didn't want to let down my Polish climbing buddy.

I clipped in and edged out on to the ledge, whacking my ice axe into the ice above me as Iwan had done. As I edged forwards, I could feel myself falling backwards.

"I'm going!" I shouted.

"Pull da vope!"

I yanked hard on it and swung back on to the ledge. I was shitting myself. I kept the rope tight and shuffled very slowly along the ledge, moving my axe 15 centimetres at a time... nearly there... nearly there... And then I was at the edge of the ledge.

Now I just had to haul myself up on to the boulder...

I pulled hard on the rope with my left hand and swung the

axe into the ice above me. I was firmly pinned to the ledge, but I couldn't move. How the hell had Iwan pulled himself up?

"I can't move!"

"Yu can! Come!" he shouted, encouragingly.

Shit. I couldn't let him down... I pulled really hard and moved my right foot up, digging the toe of the crampons into the ice – would it hold? I pulled hard with both hands and moved my left foot... Shit, this felt very unstable. I jabbed my foot in.

I was still there, hanging on – not 30 metres below.

I lifted my right foot again, pulled up and peered over the top of the boulder. Iwan was sitting there, with a grin like a Cheshire cat.

"Come!"

One last pull. I yanked with all my might, cleared the edge and rolled onto the snow on top of the boulder, gasping for air. Iwan laughed. The thought of having to go down this hellish boulder again on the way back was horrific.

By now, it was nearing seven o'clock in the morning. We didn't have much time; the sun would be rising soon and we didn't want to be hanging around in the Icefall when that happened. The warmth from the sunlight would melt and weaken the ice, causing collapses everywhere.

We carried on, arriving at the third ladder not long after. This was three buckled ladders roughly strapped together with cord, lying horizontal across a huge crevasse, with a very slack guide rope at the side.

Iwan looked for a brief second and then went. The three ladders bounced alarmingly in the middle under his lean weight. I hoped to hell they would hold mine.

Once he was across, he glanced back and nodded, and I stepped out. The ladders started to bounce. I carefully placed my crampons across two rungs at a time... one missed placement and I would be down ten metres in a second. The ladders bounced like hell as I panted madly for air and with sheer adrenalin, and the hairs prickled on the back of my neck with fear. After what seemed an eternity, I made it to the other side.

We carried on through the thick snow. We were almost there.

Soon, we reached the fourth ladder – or where the fourth ladder should have been. This area was just short of the 'football pitch', which is just below Camp 1.

Tentatively, we approached the edge of the wide, deep crevasse. In the dark depths, there was a shimmer of aluminium – the ladder had fallen way down below. The guide rope lay loosely across the gaping chasm.

"Ve go down, climb up," said Iwan. "Or ve go back."

The sun was rising – I could see the brightness in the sky. It had taken us two hours to get this far, and it would take the same to get back.

"The sun's coming up," I said.

He nodded.

"We go back."

Iwan pointed down at the mystery climber's footprints. He then pointed to the other side of the crevasse.

"He made it."

I was very impressed. This mysterious person had climbed down the crevasse and back up the other side. In my mind, this was it – this was the proof we needed. The Khumbu Icefall was passable; the route to Camp 1 was navigable. We could easily replace this ladder. The expedition could continue and we could reach our goal. Reaching the summit of Everest was now a realistic, achievable goal.

We turned back, aiming to beat the sunlight to the foot of the Icefall.

In my head, I thanked the mystery climber for helping us prove that it could be done.

We moved quickly back through the Icefall, racing the ever-advancing line of sunlight that crept across the valley towards the base of the Fall as the sun rose on the far side of Everest. The line of the sun coming up the valley felt like a horse racing towards us, competing to beat us to the bottom of the Icefall.

Before long, we saw the welcome sight of the blue SPCC tent, abandoned at the foot of the Icefall. I wondered if anybody would return to collect it, or whether it would have to endure a rough winter at Base Camp, if the monsoon season didn't destroy it.

In high spirits, we walked back through the maze of seracs to the now-familiarly dishevelled Base Camp.

We headed straight for the mess tent – it was breakfast time. We were excited to tell everybody our news, and we were also very hungry. At that altitude, the body is burning a huge amount of calories just to move, and we'd really been exerting ourselves up on the Icefall. We must have burned off the equivalent of five roast dinners.

As we entered the mess tent, Louise and John waved and beckoned us over. The guides looked up from their end of the table with raised eyebrows.

We squeezed ourselves into small spaces at the table.

"So?" said Louise.

Iwan tore into his breakfast of eggs and beans.

"We made it to the fourth ladder," I said. "We ran out of time."

"The ladders are intact?" asked a disbelieving John.

The bustle and murmur of conversation around the table had ceased. All eyes were on us. The guides looked on, untrusting.

"Three," said Iwan through a mouthful of egg.

"The other, the fourth one, has collapsed."

I saw one of the guides smirking.

"But it's passable," I added quickly. "Someone has already done it."

"Who?"

"I have no idea. We followed footprints up the Icefall; they continued on the other side of the crevasse where the ladder had collapsed."

The silence was oppressive. They waited for me to continue.

"It's passable; we can get through the Khumbu Icefall."

An eruption of chatter – questions flew at me from all sides.

"Was it easy?"

"What condition was the Icefall in?"

"Do you think we should go?"

One of the guides stood up.

"This is ridiculous," he said. Silence quickly fell. "Delusional. If it's even true that these two went up the Icefall, there are no guarantees that it is safe for all of us to go traipsing up."

"This is Everest; there are never guarantees that it's safe," I responded.

The guide looked at me as if I'd just blasphemed. He seemed shocked that somebody should question his authority.

"Look," I continued. "We've got the resources, we've got the means and we've got the will and desire to keep going. We've spent weeks acclimatising and we're just sitting around at Base Camp; we've all paid to do the one thing we're not even trying to do; reach that summit." I pointed towards Everest.

There was a murmur of agreement.

"The resources?" the guide said. "What resources? Most of the Sherpas have gone, the country's in ruins – the ice doctors are on their way to close the Icefall."

"We can persuade them not to, if they know we want to go up. If we want to keep the Icefall open, I am sure we can keep it open. There are enough Sherpas still here, looking for work. We can get them together as a team."

There were quite a lot of Sherpas that came up to EBC, not with any particular expedition, but looking for work. If they didn't find it, they were in for a very miserable winter; a lot of them relied on the income from Everest to survive. And I had heard that some Sherpas, having checked that their families down the valley were safe, had even already returned to EBC.

I could see that I was striking a chord with the team. The

idea of giving up, going back to our daily lives and not even attempting the summit would be something that would play on our consciences for the rest of our lives. There would forever be a part of us that would be thinking of Everest.

None of us wanted to endure the six-week acclimatisation, wracking coughs and headaches again – the long, cold trek up the valley, sleeping in draughty coffin tents in the freezing nights. And some could not afford to come again; this was their only chance. We were here, we were all in good physical condition; we were ready for it.

"The team all want to climb," I said.

"It's not up to you," the guide retorted. He'd already mentally checked out of EBC.

There it was, the simple truth – it wasn't up to us. There was no democracy at Everest Base Camp. But I felt we should all have a say.

We had all taken two months away from our families and our loved ones, and we really didn't want to have to come back again. The Icefall was passable and I felt it would be the wrong decision to give up now. I decided it was time for a pause and a careful think.

I left the mess tent, my breakfast barely touched.

Louise followed.

"Jules," she shouted after me as I trekked away across the snow-covered landscape.

I stopped and waited for her to catch up.

"Is that it?"

"Until I get on a helicopter and leave Base Camp, I won't

believe that that's it, but it's time to reflect and gauge the mood of the rest of the team."

"Good – I want to keep going, too."

That filled me full of hope – Louise wanted to keep going. I thought that, if I could muster enough support within our team and across EBC from the remnants of other expeditions, maybe we could persuade the Icefall doctors to keep the mountain open and repair the fallen ladders.

It was exhausting work, trucking across Base Camp, talking to people and canvassing opinion. I mean, it was difficult enough due to the terrain, but the thin air meant that I was panting all the time. On a scrap of paper, I jotted down the details of people willing to crack on and attempt the summit.

I was feeling good physically. No Buddha's Revenge, my feet were in good nick. I felt ready to give the mountain a crack. I'd lost a lot of weight – my trousers were loose – but I didn't realise that at the time. Your body starts eating itself at altitude; the calorific content required to keep warm and functional is enormous.

In the days following the disaster, I had been speaking to one of the other camp leaders. He was more open to the idea of summiting, so I headed off to find him. I jumped straight into the conversation.

"Would you still consider going up?" I asked bluntly.

He looked up at me, taking me in, considering me.

"If people still have the will to; sure," he replied.

"People do still have the will."

He indicated an empty chair next to him; I sat down.

"Look, the simple fact is if we've got the supplies. We just need the people and the guides. If you bring all that together, you've got an expedition. If you can get me a list of people willing to go, as well as a sufficient number of Sherpas – who are *willing* to go – then I would consider it."

I had the beginnings of a list, screwed up in my pocket. I started to feel hopeful, confident again.

"How many Sherpas do we need?"

"It depends on how many climbers you've got."

He looked up at Everest, shielding his eyes from the sun.

"You've not got long, either," he said calmly. "Get me the list in 24 hours and I *might* be able to get an expedition together. I emphasise 'might' – some things I can't control."

I thanked him, shook his hand and stood up.

"Come and find me tomorrow," he said. "Let me know how you've done."

I nodded and walked off.

"Oh," he shouted after me, "I would suggest trying at the Indian Army's camp. Rumour is they're still keen. That's also where you'll find the ice doctors."

He waved at me casually, before returning to scratching his beard.

I began my journey back to our camp, adding names to my list as I went. When I arrived, I saw Iwan chatting to Petar, the Polish father. I headed straight over.

They were speaking quickly. Although I couldn't understand what they were saying, it sounded serious.

"Everything ok?"

Petar looked at me, through panicky, tear-washed eyes.

"His son," Iwan said. "His footprints."

His footprints?

I thought back to the Icefall, to the mystery footprints through the perilous route. His son?

"It was him?"

Iwan nodded.

"Went to get equipment from Cump 1."

"On his own?"

Iwan handed me a note, written in Polish. The script was shaky, rushed.

"What does it say?"

"'Father – I go to get equipment from Camp 1. I am sorry. I love you' – found it this morning, inside son's tent."

Petar began speaking again, his voice filled with concern. Iwan attempted to calm him.

"He is worried," said Iwan simply. "Vants to go up now."

"Now? That's crazy. We can go in the morning."

"Ve?" said Iwan, smiling slightly.

"Of course, 'we'".

"I was hoping you say dis".

Iwan told Petar that it would be impossible to go now – far too dangerous. He assured him that we would go in the morning, the three of us. We would climb up to Camp 1, or somewhere where we could contact the son.

We assured him Andrzej would be fine. He was an experienced climber; we had seen his footprints continuing beyond the last crevasse. We could help him bring some of the gear down.

We arranged to meet the following morning at the foot of the Icefall at 5am, earlier than we had that day, in order to give us more time to reach the top.

I thought about how I would feel, helplessly sitting by while one of my daughters was in a dangerous situation. I would want everybody to help. I felt very sorry for the dad – it was now my turn to help him.

I forgot all about the list.

The Icefall revisited; the expedition in peril

My watch alarm buzzed into life at 4am. It was freezing cold, with icicles on the inside of my tent, and pitch black. I was very tired. I tentatively pushed a hand out of my downing sleeping bag. Boy, it was cold! I rummaged in the side pocket for my head torch. Oh, jeepers, what *had* I agreed to do?

After our conversation with Petar the previous evening, Iwan had gone to see Donald to tell him what he planned to do. But Donald had had a change of heart. He had been warned by his sponsors that it would not look good for him to go ahead with the climb, so he could no longer support Iwan's going up the Icefall. Apparently, there was a big argument, and Iwan had been forced to drop the idea.

So Iwan wouldn't be coming this morning. It was now up to me alone to help Petar, with whom I couldn't even communicate, to find his son. If it had been one of my daughters, I would have been desperate for somebody to help me. That's the way I rationalised it, although I knew it was insanely dangerous.

After I found out that Iwan couldn't come, I had sought out Petar to assure him I would still help him. One of the guides had interrupted us.

"We need you to sign this," he had said.

"What is it?"

"A disclaimer form."

"Disclaimer for what?"

"If you're really going up the Icefall again, we need you to sign this. We can't be held responsible if you go and hurt yourself."

I laughed. This is what it had come to! They wanted to make sure they were under no obligation to come and rescue me if I got injured.

The whole expedition team seemed to be crumbling under the stress.

I took the form, glanced over it.

"We can still summit," I said, as I signed it. "We haven't all given up yet."

It was pretty clear that the guides had checked out – they spent their time at Base Camp smoking dope, drinking and discussing their plans for Thailand. One of them had already booked his flights.

"Sure," the guide replied with a smirk, taking the signed form from me and walking off.

I had my doubts as to whether we would ever go up. I really did have my doubts by that stage – everything seemed to be against it.

In the gloomy darkness of the early morning, I dressed myself and crawled out of the tent.

I headed over to the mess tent and peered inside – no

familiar, smiley face of Iwan this time. It was a very quiet, very eerie stillness. Nothing was moving – not even the ghosts of the dead climbers. The hairs on the back of my neck prickled as I shoved Weetabix down, filled my water bottle and left camp to meet Petar at the SPCC tent.

My head torch created eerie, haunting shadows as I walked, and I found myself thinking about all the people who had died here – not just this year, but throughout history...

It was pitch black, nothing was moving. There were no birds this high up. No creatures could live up here. There was just silence – a silence quite unlike anything I'd ever experienced before, an oppressive, constricting, haunting silence.

I wondered how many lives Everest has taken; how many orphans, widows she had created. I felt as if the spirits of all those lost souls whirled and drifted around me, delicately held aloft by the freezing wind.

I heard a trickling sound, the sound of running water – the stream in the glacier. I was planning on following the thin, meandering stream to the foot of the Icefall again.

It took around 30 minutes to make it to the foot of the Icefall. The gloom was beginning to lift as the valley became lighter. This wasn't the sun; the light came up first, several hours before the warm sunlight follows.

I saw the blue canvas of the SPCC tent, but no sign of any human life.

"Hello?" I shouted.

Perhaps he'd gone? Perhaps he didn't have confidence in me and he'd gone ahead. Maybe he couldn't wait any longer to see if his son was alive.

"Hello? Hello?" My voice echoed off into the eerie silence of the huge seracs around me.

I shouted for around five minutes or so. Was the Pole actually coming ?

"Hello!" shot a voice through the darkness, at last.

I saw a figure around 40 metres away, approaching me. He was a small, wiry man, but with many years' climbing experience.

As he approached, I could hear the ice crunching under his crampons.

"I late, I late," he said, shaking his head.

"No worries," I replied. "Let's go."

He nodded enthusiastically. I led the way.

We didn't rope ourselves together this time; we just clipped in our jumars and climbed. We followed the same route I had taken with Iwan the day before.

I was very impressed by Petar. His pace was so steady, so constant; a beautiful pace. He was 66, but he moved up that mountain like a much younger man. And then there was me, five steps, then on my hands and knees gasping for oxygen! Still, I felt proud that I was able to try to help him, to offer support as we made our way up the Icefall.

We reached the first ladder, still intact, and crossed. The same with the second. We came to the third...

Petar looked at me. His expression was easy enough to read: *will that hold*?

I nodded, clipped onto the dangling rope and proceeded to

cross the very bouncy trio of ladders. It was daunting, but I just got on with it. He followed, and we headed upwards.

Then there was the boulder and the ledge with its 30m drop to negotiate. We climbed along the ledge around the side of the bolder, ice axes in hand hacking away at the ice as we went.

Eventually, we arrived at the fourth ladder, just short of the 'football pitch'. We were now not far from Camp 1. This was where the last ladder point had collapsed.

We walked to the edge and looked down at the twisted aluminium, many metres below.

The safety rope was still in place, hanging across the crevasse, but with no knowledge of the anchor at the other side it was not safe to use.

There was no way we could cross the crevasse unless we climbed all the way down and then ice-climbed out with twin ice axes. But we didn't have twin axes; we only had one ice axe each.

My companion's son had climbed down – on his own – and then climbed back up the other side to continue onwards. I had profound admiration for him; the nerve that he had to go and do that by himself. I mean it was stupid, yeah, but this man had balls... I mean, titanium balls, and huge ones at that. You had to admire the guy. It was incredible.

Without twin axes we could not climb down the crevasse and back out. We tried for a while to find a route around the crevasse, using our ropes to try to get across, but it was impossible. We were running out of time, the sun was beginning to rise.

In the end, we used one of the ice doctors' clips to anchor me, and I belayed Petar down the crevasse, to see if he could find a route up the other side without twin axes, but he couldn't, so I helped him climb back to me.

I could see the look of dejection on his face.

We were now very close to Camp 1, so there was a chance he might be able to make contact with his son on their two-way radios.

He turned it on and tried... All we could hear was a faint crackle. He tried again... crackle, crackle... He kept going.

A faint voice came through – the voice of Andrzej.

Petar's face lit up, and he shouted into the radio. This was the first sign that he had had in 36 hours that his son was still alive. The relief in his voice was clearly audible. They chatted for about 30 seconds – a difficult, stilted, conversation, due to the terrible reception.

"Do you want a helicopter rescue for your son?" I asked.

He wanted to call the camp, to speak to Donat or Iwan. He tried on his radio – with no luck.

Our choices were limited. Either we carry on to Camp 1 and stay there, or head back down again... I was risking my life here now – really risking my life. The sun was rising and the ice was beginning to melt. Climbing into that crevasse without twin ice axes was a fool's errand...

I thought about Steph and Lizzie... We were beyond the boundaries of sensible stuff now. I was endangering myself for somebody else's child. And although I was very glad to help, I did not want to deprive my children of their father.

I had my radio, but it was not the same as the Polish radios, so it was no use for contacting Andrzej, but I was able to contact Base Camp. One of the guides answered.

"Look, maybe he needs a helicopter rescue for his son."

The guide was less than helpful.

"There's not much we can do."

"Please get me Donat or Iwan. They need to speak to the Polish guy."

Soon, Donat's voice came over the radio. Petar was eager to talk to him, so I passed the radio over.

They chatted away in Polish for a minute or two: double Dutch to me.

Donat spoke to me.

"He OK – the son. He no rush – he have breakfast. In two hour he come down."

My heart lifted. I had true admiration for Andrzej – in spite of the earthquake and avalanche, as well as the unknown conditions, he had climbed solo up to Camp 1, to get their equipment. A lot of the climb would have been in the dark, and he had spent the night there alone. Now, he was relaxing cooking himself breakfast, with no rush – it was impressive.

"That's great news!"

I felt as if a weight had been lifted from me. There was no reason to go any further; we could head back to Base Camp knowing that Petar's son was safe. He would come down shortly, and once he was safely back at Base Camp, everything would be fine. I now felt I had done my bit to help father make contact with son, and there was no shame in turning around.

Also, I had now been this far up the Icefall twice, and Andrzej had made it all the way to Camp 1. This proved it was possible – so, hopefully, we could carry on with our expedition now.

Petar hugged me, laughing. There was a huge smile on his face and a real glint in his eyes – the eyes of a very relieved and proud father. Although his son had done a stupid thing going up on his own, he had actually made it to Camp 1.

So we turned and made our way back down the Icefall. We left the rope that we had secured at the fourth ladder and used to belay Petar into the crevasse, so that Andrzej would be able to use it on his return.

A huge ice serac had collapsed across the route between our going up and coming down. It had shattered into a million pieces and buried the rope beneath it. It had looked quite stable earlier, but now it was smashed into tiny pieces, with a few very large chunks lying around. If that had come down on our heads, it would have killed us both outright.

We had to shimmy around the ice that now blocked the route, with our backs to the wall...

I couldn't have a sensible conversation with Petar about the pros and cons of squeezing ourselves through that gap between the huge fallen serac and the crevasse wall, because he didn't speak enough English. Instead, I just had to get on with it; get on with the madness.

I went first, taking off my rucksack and pulling it behind me as I inched my way through – the walls were pressing against my chest. I felt very claustrophobic, and I was praying there would be no aftershocks that might dislodge any of the ice. Any slight movement of the ice and it could have crushed me to death.

I made it through the cavity and Petar followed. As he was about to clear the gap, we heard an almighty crack.

We both froze.

A large chunk of ice dislodged itself. It smashed to the ground, inches from our feet, showering us with freezing ice.

"Quick," I said.

He nodded, hauled himself out of the gap, and we increased our speed of descent, eager to get out of the melting Icefall before it killed us. The sun had risen by this point, beating down on us and threatening to bring more ice down around us.

Eventually, panting, exhausted, we reached the relative safety of the glacier floor. We stood near the SPCC tent gasping for breath.

"Thank...you..." Petar said, between huge gulps of thin air.

I patted him on the back. I felt proud to have helped him in my small way. It was great to know that his son was safe and would hopefully be back at Base Camp shortly. I thought about my daughters and hoped that, if we were ever in a comparable situation, someone would help me to rescue them.

On a personal level, I also felt I had climbed part of Everest twice now, having been up the Khumbu Icefall two days in a row.

The Icefall was passable; I knew that. Andrzej had climbed it, and we could, too – we just needed to go earlier, avoiding the sunlight and the melting ice, and carve a new route around the fourth ladder, or put it back into place, and we could get to Camp 1.

I was very excited to get back to Base Camp and tell the others.

* * * * *

As we were walking back to Base Camp, we saw three men approaching us. They appeared to be heading in the direction of the Icefall.

At this time of day? Were they crazy?

As they got closer, I could see that one of them was wearing a blue helmet with SPCC emblazoned on the front in large, white letters.

"Where you come from?"

These were the mystical Icefall doctors, who set the route through the Icefall with ropes and ladders each year.

"From near the football pitch," I replied.

"No. Impossible. No ladders," one of them said, as we stopped to chat.

"Yes there are. The first three ladders are fine," I said. "It's just the fourth one that's collapsed."

It seemed they had been listening to the false rumours that the route through the icefall was impassable.

"What are you guys doing?" I asked them. "Are you repairing the route through the Icefall?"

"No. We remove ladders."

I thought about Andrzej, calmly sitting at Camp 1 having breakfast. If they removed the ladders, he would be stranded.

"You can't do that. There's somebody at Camp 1," I said.

"No, no – impossible."

They looked genuinely shocked.

"Somebody climbed up to Camp 1 yesterday. He's coming back down this morning," I explained.

"Our manager said remove ladders."

Petar, even with his limited English, appeared to understand what was going on.

"Son," he said, pointing towards Camp 1.

I patted his back.

"You can't remove the ladders; his son is still at Camp 1."

"We have instruction."

"He won't be able to get down!"

I was exhausted after our climb.

The Icefall doctors were Nepalese, but they spoke reasonable English. I tried to explain the situation – that Andrzej needed the ladders to get back down, otherwise he would be stranded up at Camp 1 with no way of getting back.

This was my main concern, but in addition, if they took the ladders down, our summit attempt was over. We would have no hope of continuing. And most of our team seemed keen to carry on.

"Our boss..."

"I don't care what your boss said. If you take those ladders down now, somebody else could die."

There was silence. The SPCC guys looked uncomfortable.

They shared nervous glances.

"We leave ladders. Talk to boss."

"Good."

It was fortunate that we had bumped into the SPCC men. Otherwise, they would have removed the ladders, and Andrzej would have been stranded. I looked at Petar, trying to reassure him that his son wouldn't be left halfway up Everest to fend for himself, or wait for a helicopter rescue which they couldn't afford.

I felt sorry for the SPCC men. They were just pawns in this process, doing what their manager told them. They risked their lives every year to make the route through the Icefall safe for us.

We trudged on, leaving the SPCC guys to return to their tents.

We arrived back at the perimeter of Base Camp at around 11 in the morning. Petar was camped at the top end of Base Camp, while I was at the bottom. He had a large smile on his face as he hugged me.

"*Dziekuje* – thank you," he said.

"Let me know when your son gets down," I replied, slowly pointing at Camp 1 and then moving my finger down to Base Camp, hoping that he understood what I was saying.

He nodded, and we went our separate ways, waving to each other. (I heard later that Andrzej did successfully come back down the Icefall, taking six hours instead of the usual two, because of all the heavy equipment he was carrying with him. He had risked crossing it when it was at its most treacherous

– in the middle of the day – but had survived unscathed.)

I felt a warm glow – I had climbed the Icefall again, which I had actually really enjoyed, I had made Petar happy, and we had prevented the Icefall doctors from removing the ladders before his son got down.

All in all, it was a very good morning's work.

I walked back along the stream in the glacier to our camp. Very few people now remained, and I did not see anybody on my way back.

It was just over a week since the avalanche. While a lot of the debris had been removed, reclaimed or rebuilt, there were still unclaimed items scattered everywhere.

I passed a piece of plastic jutting out of the snow. I grabbed it with my gloved hand and yanked it free – a laptop!

It almost certainly didn't work, having been outside in freezing temperatures for a week. I placed it on a nearby rock. Somebody might want it, and I didn't know what else to do with it.

Soon, I was walking into the white pod. There was a faint chatter of voices.

I looked around the pod – it was quite amazing how much could change within a week.

There had been a great sense of camaraderie before the disaster. Now, our group seemed fractured, broken, divided. The guides kept to themselves, Lincoln, with his broad welcoming smile, was gone, Iwan and Donat kept their distance from Donald. It was a completely different place.

The night before the avalanche we had had a party, right

here in the white pod.

The guides, Louise, John, Donald, Paul, Lincoln, Elia, Hilary, Iwan, Donat, Hachiro, Taka, Bill and I – we had all danced the night away. Happy, excited, enthusiastic, looking forward to our big adventure up Everest.

That was before the earthquake.

Now, I sat down with Louise and John, who were seated in the reclining chairs to the right of the pod.

"We can do it," I said. "The Icefall is passable."

"He's back," said Louise.

"Who?"

"The expedition leader."

The expedition leader had pretty much left us to our own devices since we arrived at Base Camp. He'd left the day-to-day running of the expedition to his guides and had gone back to Kathmandu before the earthquake. We hadn't seen him for eight days.

"When did he get back?"

"This morning," said John. "He went to see the Icefall doctors straight away. He hasn't even come to say hello to us."

That would be why they were off to close the Icefall then. If he had pressured them to take the ladders down, they'd give in pretty quickly.

"Where are they?"

"Who?" asked Louise.

"The Icefall doctors. Where can I find them?"

"They usually hang out at the Indian Army camp," said Louise. "But why?"

"I'm going to go and talk to them," I said, standing up. "The Icefall is still passable. You still want to try don't you?"

Louise and John looked at each other.

"Of course we do," said Louise. "It's why we're still here."

"Exactly. If we can put pressure on the doctors to keep the ladders in place, and we find some willing Sherpas to assist us, we can still go. We can still try and summit Everest."

"They're not going to be happy about that," said Louise, her eye shifting over to the guides sitting across on the far side of the pod. The pod was some 10 metres across, so they couldn't hear us.

"They've been trying to find any reason to avoid going up and doing what we've paid them to do. It doesn't matter to them – they still get full pay whether we go or not, and if we don't, they spend the next three weeks lying on a beach with some Thai girls."

Louise and John smiled.

"I'm going to find the Icefall doctors," I said, spinning on my heel and leaving the white pod.

Duplicity
and dashed hopes

It was a 30-minute hike right across BC to the top end, then, after asking five people, I eventually found the Indian Army's camp. The Indian Army was one of the few full-strength expeditions remaining, with some 25 people. The army comes every year with soldiers to climb Everest. I assume it must be part of their training programme.

The Indians were very welcoming, very lovely. As soon as I arrived, I was greeted.

"Hello, my friend!" said an Indian officer in impeccable English. They were wearing thick downing clothing, much like the rest of us, but with army insignia stitched to the arms and lapels.

I didn't waste time.

"I'm from another expedition," I said. "We still want to climb."

The Indian officer looked at me, as if assessing my merits.

"You had better come with me then," he said, putting an arm around my shoulders and leading me into a tent. "I'll introduce you to Ank."

We walked into the tent where a large number of Indians and Nepalese were sitting around a very large table that filled the middle of the tent. There was also a Westerner with a ponytail and a bright orange jacket, a Belgian called Damien. I learned that he had been with another expedition, which had left BC, but Damien wanted to stay and try for the summit, so the Indian Army had kindly offered him food and a tent in its camp.

Some people were eating in the tent. "You must join us and eat something." They thrust a silver dish into my hand full of samosas, rice and *dal bhat*. It looked and smelled delicious. I sensed a camaraderie here that no longer existed in our own camp.

There was a very large Nepalese man sitting across the table, who seemed to fill the tent.

"This man and his expedition still want to climb," the officer said.

The large man had the air of an important official. He looked up from his seated position, his face serious and composed. This was the Icefall boss – Ank.

"I have asked my team to remove ladders, ropes, everything," he said.

"I know – I saw them when I was coming down the Icefall. You can't take them down, though. There's still somebody at Camp 1."

The large man raised an eyebrow

"You went up the Icefall?"

"Yes."

Silence had fallen in the tent – everybody seemed interested in the outcome of this conversation.

"I have been told it is not passable," Ank said.

"That's not true. I've been up it twice, seen it with my own eyes. Three of the ladders are intact."

He seemed to weigh up this new information.

"In our expedition," I continued, "there are nine of us who want to carry on. There are also five from the South African team. Plus these guys…" I gesticulated towards the Indians. I had sensed their keenness as I talked. The Indian officer nodded seriously.

"We still wish to go up," he said.

"There's a lot of people here at BC who want to give it a shot, to try and achieve their dream. We've all paid for our permits, the route is accessible and we're all in good shape, already acclimatised. We ask for your support to achieve our dreams." I knew I said it with an air of desperation, although I was trying to keep my voice steady.

I showed him pictures of the Icefall from my camera.

"I was told it was worse – that only one ladder remained," he conceded.

"There are three."

"You need the Sherpa support," he said.

"I understand that."

"It will take many Sherpas to make the route from Camp 1 to the summit. Can you find 16 Sherpas willing to go? You must not pressurise them, and they must be willing to go," he emphasised.

"With our expedition, the Indian Army, and the South Africans, I think I can."

He paused, went silent, seemed to freeze in place like a great Buddha statue.

"If you demonstrate this to me," he paused for what seemed like an age, "I will reopen the Icefall."

The whole tent lit up. I saw huge grins on the faces of the Indian Army men, including their captain. There was real hope here again. I shook his hand, thanked him and stood up. He nodded.

"Bring me 16 Sherpas willing to go," he repeated.

The Indian Army officer led me out of the tent. As he pulled back the flap, he shook my hand.

"Well done," he said. "Well done – we still have a chance."

"We do," I said. "And thank you for your kind hospitality and support."

I headed back to our camp, another 30-minute, breathless trek across rough, uneven ice and rocks. It was now past midday, and I'd been up since four in the morning. I was very tired. The adrenalin had been pumping for hours, first with the Icefall, and now with this renewed opportunity, and I was intensely thirsty, but I had to give this my best shot. With the expedition leader back, he was the last person I had to persuade, and then we could have a real shot at the summit...

In spite of my exhaustion, I was going to give it my all to corral the teams for the rest of the day.

Eventually, I reached the white pod. I opened the entrance flap and stepped inside.

"That's it then – meeting closed."

The expedition leader was sitting in a chair in the centre of the white pod, with the guides beside him. The rest of the expedition team was seated in front of him.

"What meeting?" I said from the entrance.

"I'm afraid you've missed it," said the expedition leader.

"Nobody told me there was a meeting!"

"You weren't here."

"I was here earlier. You were around this morning and you didn't even say hello to anybody, and now you're suddenly telling me that there was a meeting planned! You could have told me this morning and I would have come to it."

I felt betrayed. I knew this meeting was to close down the expedition, and I knew they had made little attempt to tell people about the meeting in the hope that there would be fewer people to object. I felt they had deliberately avoided telling me, to try to sideline me.

"I understand you weren't here this morning, anyway."

"I was up the Icefall, but I was back at 11 o'clock. I saw your guides then, and they didn't say anything about a meeting. What did you decide? I'm part of this expedition; I think I've got a right to know."

"It's not safe. The Icefall isn't safe, so the Icefall doctors have decided to close the mountain," said the expedition leader.

"No," I retorted. "That isn't true, that isn't true. I have just been to speak to the Icefall doctors – I spoke to Ank!"

As I said this, the expedition leader jumped out of his

chair. I thought he was going to come and clock me one. He was clearly hopping mad. I think the idea that one of his expedition team members could have the audacity to go to speak to the Icefall doctors directly without his permission was, to him, unthinkable. And then to speak back to him and question his decision...that was unheard of. But we were an expedition team – we all had a right to say what we thought about the future of the expedition and to have input into the final decision.

The members of the team were all highly successful people, a heart surgeon, an actuary, another doctor, a fighter pilot, an entrepreneur, etc. We were being treated like kids. There was no real leadership from the top; it was more of a dictatorship. It showed an overall lack of management, and, consequently, there was dissent in the ranks. It was a horrible discordant environment to be in.

In reality, it was all about money. I was aware that the expedition leader had already paid out $100,000 for the two kilometres of rope that are required from Camp 2 to the summit. Normally, the bigger expeditions all chip in together for the rope before the season starts. These expeditions are not known for their financial management, and I heard that our expedition hadn't billed the others before the season started.

Of course, the other expeditions had now left, so they were hardly likely to turn around and pay for the rope. Our expedition leader was in line to make a big loss on the rope if he used it. That's what it all came down to, at the end of the day; it all came down to money. He wasn't willing to make a loss, so instead, we, the expedition members, had to.

"I have been told that the Icefall isn't safe," he shouted bullishly. I could see the effort that it was taking him to restrain himself.

"That's not true," I said, unflinchingly. "I've been up this morning, I can show you the pictures. There are three good ladders – we can do it. I chatted to Ank, the manager of the Icefall doctors, and he said that if we could find 16 willing Sherpas, then he'd open the Icefall. After six weeks here, in these freezing conditions, I think it's only fair that we're allowed to have a crack at it."

The expedition leader looked at me. I could see he was furious that I was daring to challenge his authority. I suspect nobody had ever really done that to him before. But I also knew I had presented new information – and that there was now a real opportunity to continue.

The rest of the tent was silent – you could hear a pin drop.

The expedition leader changed tactic.

"It isn't safe above the Icefall. What about Camp 1 to 2? Camp 2 to 3? They aren't safe, either."

"How do you know that?" I asked. "You haven't been up there; nobody has been up there. The last time you climbed Everest was 1998. How do you know what's up there? You don't; that's a ridiculous comment."

"It won't be safe up there – the earthquake will have done some damage."

"It's Everest! It's never going to be *safe*; if it was *safe* then none of us would be here!"

He seemed to realise I wasn't going to be a pushover.

"OK," he said. "It's very dangerous, and we are not sure we can make it. Does anyone else still want to go up?" I had to admire him for opening up the debate.

There was a deadly silence for a few seconds. The group was afraid to challenge him.

"Louise does," I said, hoping to get the debate going.

"Yes, I do," she said. "I did not succeed last year, I just want a chance at the summit."

"Paul?"

"I'll be guided by our leader."

John also left judgment to the expedition leader, but the two Japanese, Hachiro and Taka, as well as Donat and Iwan, all still wanted to go.

Bearing in mind that this was a controversial situation, I thought we had a good result. Out of the nine remaining members of our expedition, none of them had said that they definitely did not want to go. Everyone was willing to give it a shot...if the expedition leader was willing.

"It's my decision," he said, playing his trump card, "and my decision is final. It's too dangerous. We are not going up."

And that was that.

I knew there was no point arguing further. He'd taken our money with the promise we would attempt to summit Everest, and I understood that sometimes it would be out of his control, but that wasn't the case here; we had the opportunity and he'd decided against taking it.

The meeting ended, the expedition leader talked to his

guides in harsh whispers and then headed out of the white pod in the direction of the Indian Army camp.

I had no doubt that he was off to see Ank, the Icefall doctor, to get the Icefall closed for good.

One of the guides told us to pack our bags, as we'd be leaving in the morning for the three-day trek out.

I felt numb, completely exhausted and drained. It was over. I had given it my all. I had talked and cajoled everybody I could. I don't think I could have done more. The carpet had been ripped from under my feet, and all hope had gone.

I felt a great wave of exhaustion sweep over me.

Now, suddenly, I wanted to get out of this place as soon as possible. There was no reason to be here any longer; if we weren't going up Everest, I was going home.

I wanted to see my daughters, and hold them tightly in my arms again. Thoughts of them had filled many of my waking hours at BC and now I would see them again soon. I was very happy about that, at least; it was compensation.

The discontentment was palpable among the expedition team. The guides had all left the tent, and we were left to discuss what had just happened.

"It's over then," said Paul.

No one said much. Hachiro was talking to Taka very quickly in Japanese; I think he was explaining what had just happened. Donat and Iwan sat stony-faced at the back of the tent.

Later, we all sat in the mess tent, eating our final evening meal together at BC. The guides had decided to eat in the other mess tent, and we, the remaining nine, were in the second mess tent, which suited us just fine.

We thanked Bill for another great meal, and we raised a glass of lukewarm lemon tea to our failed expedition. I looked from face to face, and could see we were all in a bad place.

I glanced at Louise; her eyes were sunken, dark. She had spent 14 years preparing for Everest, and this was her second failed attempt. She was gutted.

"I was willing to put another $50,000 in if it helped, but I'm not coming back," she had said to me through tearful eyes earlier. "That's it; I'm done."

Her dream had been ripped from her once again, and she had finally given up on it. I really felt for her. My decision to come had been a quick one, but she had spent 14 years preparing.

There was a rustling as the mess tent flap opened up, letting a breath of freezing air whip through the tent. The expedition leader walked in and sat down with us. He sat down right next to me.

I was too tired to talk to him as he tried to rebuild the bridges he had incinerated earlier in the day. I felt I might say something I'd regret if I said anything at all.

We were all done. We had all accepted that we weren't going to attempt the summit.

Unavoidably, we got into conversation about the Icefall. The expedition leader repeated his false claim that it was impassable, and that the Icefall doctors had taken the decision to close it.

"That's not the case!" I said, almost incredulously. "I told you earlier they were willing to keep it open if we found 16 Sherpas!"

"That's not true," he replied.

"What do you mean it's not true? I was there this afternoon, in the Indian Army's tent, speaking to Ank."

"No, that's not true."

"What do you mean it's not true? Are you calling me a liar?" I asked.

"Yes," he shot me a look as cold as the snow. "You're lying."

I was gobsmacked. It had descended to this level now. I had no reason to lie – there was absolutely no point in my lying about anything – but now this guy, on top of everything else, on top of taking my money and cancelling the expedition, was calling me a liar.

I bit my lip. I had no more to say.

I turned to my left to talk to Louise.

"I'm so disappointed," she said.

After dinner, I went straight to bed.

In the morning, I would be going home.

An unexpectedly easy exit

It was a three-day trek down the Khumbu Valley.

As I awoke, the events of the previous night surged through me like a tidal wave of nausea. It was all over – we were going back down.

I sat up in my coffin for the last time. I had mixed feelings. On the one hand, I was going home to my daughters and I couldn't wait to see them again, I also wouldn't have to sleep in that bloody coffin at -15 degrees again. On the other hand, all that preparation was for nothing; my dream of climbing Everest was over.

The sunlight penetrated the yellow-orange canvas of the tent. I dressed and crawled out, looking back at the tent. The expedition's logo was proudly printed on the side.

I grabbed a cup of Her Maj's finest – it was still the finest, even though we were leaving – and a piece of toast, and headed back to my tent to pack my gear into my two expedition bags. I put my electrical items into my rucksack. Gentle as they are, I didn't trust a yak with my electrical gear; I was going to carry that in the rucksack on my back, along with some water, my warm jacket and a book.

I tried to avoid looking up the Icefall towards Everest, now that it was all over. I tried to avoid thinking about how I would have felt at the top – it would have been amazing, incredible; it would have been indescribable. In the clear, warm sunlight, it all looked so doable.

Now, with my rucksack on my back, lugging the two kit bags to the mess tent to be loaded onto yaks, all I felt was despondency, disappointment. I felt I'd wasted a whole load of time and money on nothing.

I stood near the white pod, pausing for thought. What would the girls think? Would they understand, or would they be disappointed? Would they be ashamed, having to go into school and tell all their friends that their father had failed to summit Everest?

I wanted to be able to return home and tell them that I'd done this amazing thing. I knew no one would criticise me, because of the earthquake and avalanche, but still...

I was dreading it...but also I couldn't wait to see them again.

People were milling around, strapping bags to yaks, saying awkward, surreal farewells and heading down the valley.

Once my bags were securely fastened onto one of the gentle, stinking great beasts, I left Base Camp. There was no sentimentality; I just walked off over the ice and rocks in the direction of the valley without looking back. I didn't think I'd miss it – the frozen, sleepless nights, the coffin tent, the shit-stained, stinking toilets – and I didn't want to look at Everest any longer. I just left. I wasn't looking forward to a three-day trek, and all the discussions about "if only". I just wanted to get home.

As I left BC, I saw a man in a bright orange jacket with a long ponytail dangling down his back. It was the guy from the Indian Army tent from the previous day.

"Hey, Damien?" I said as I approached.

He turned, beamed a wide smile at me.

"Jules!" His Belgian accent made my name sound alien.

He thrust out his hand and shook mine warmly. I fell in line, walking along next to him.

As our expedition leader had decided to call it quits, the Icefall had been closed, and the dreams of the Indian Army and the South Africans were also destroyed. So the Indian Army, and Damien, were trekking out and heading home.

"I'm sorry," I said. "Sorry I couldn't persuade them."

For some reason, I felt a burden of guilt, as if my failure to convince our expedition leader had resulted in the closure of the mountain.

"It is not your fault," Damien replied. "He came back. He was red-faced, furious."

"Who?"

"Your expedition leader – I don't know what you said, but you certainly made him mad."

Damien laughed, a deep, booming laugh.

"He burst into the Indian Army tent," he continued, "went straight up to Ank and said that he had spent $100,000 on the rope, and that if anyone wanted to climb, they would have to pay for it."

I was shocked.

"The Indian Army? And those South Africans?" I asked.

"Yep. He said for each it was $8,000 if they wanted to climb."

Everybody knew the soldiers in the Indian Army couldn't afford to pay $8,000 each. We were all being held to ransom as a result of poor financial management.

Damien and I laughed about how ridiculous the situation had become, the dissolution of our small society in such a short space of time.

I liked Damien; I liked the guy's drive and enthusiasm. I liked the fact that he'd stayed behind with the Indian Army, and that he didn't give in easily.

We chatted for a little while longer, then I bade him farewell, and headed off to try to catch up with my team.

I arrived at Gorak Shep after another 45 minutes of hard trekking, stopping there for a rest and a cup of lemon tea. I needed to send some emails and the telephone mast loomed directly above me, surprisingly unharmed by earthquake or avalanche.

As I entered the cold lodge, I was delighted to spot Paul, John and Louise sitting in the corner, wrapped in their thick coats, clutching cups of steaming tea, I went over and sat down.

The mood was lighter than yesterday, not difficult, and we chatted while we rested and drank tea. I sent some emails home to the girls and to Vicky, telling them I was on my way back, paying the lodge the obligatory $5 for the privilege.

We didn't know what the situation was further down the valley or in Kathmandu. We had heard that 7,000 people had died. We had also heard there was wide-scale devastation in Kathmandu, with many buildings in ruins. I felt extremely sorry for the Nepalese. They are a very kind and gentle people, and in my short time in Nepal, I had come to love and respect them dearly. And their country was now in ruins. We had also heard that aid from other countries could not get into Nepal.

Against this backdrop, I somehow had to get home. I imagined this would be no small task. We didn't even know if the airport was still open or whether it would be running commercial flights. Perhaps I would have to cross the border to get a flight. I asked Vicky to book me any available flight at all, even if it was in the wrong direction. I could start working my way home from wherever it landed. The journey ahead might be a long one.

Just as I was finishing sending emails, I caught a glimpse of bright orange in my peripheral vision. I looked up and saw Damien enter the lodge, pull off a beanie and look around.

"Hey, Damien," I shouted. "Everybody, this is Damien – he was with the Indian Army, wanting to summit as well. These are my expedition mates and good friends: Louise, Paul and John."

Damien beamed a big smile and sat down at our table. We all had some soup to try to warm up, and chatted some more. There was a good camaraderie between the five of us.

"Damien," I said, "You remember my coming to the Indian Army tent yesterday, yes? You remember what Ank said to me about getting some Sherpas?"

"Yes," he replied. "Ank said if you could find 16 willing

Sherpas then he would reopen the Icefall."

I turned to Louise.

"You see, I wasn't lying. That is exactly what Ank said."

She looked at me with warm eyes.

"Jules, I never doubted you for a minute. I know you tried your hardest for all of us."

There was a lull in the conversation.

"You know folks," said Damien, breaking the temporary silence, "because I am Belgian, and because there has been an earthquake, this is now classified as a national disaster."

We waited for him to continue.

"Under our government's policy, any insurer has to carry out an emergency recovery for me."

Emergency recovery?

"How does that work?" I asked

"Because it is a national disaster, the Belgian government policy means that the insurance company has to come and get me. They are sending a helicopter for me."

"Woah, that's cool, so they're coming to get you now?"

"Yes," he grinned. "And, folks, there is a spare place if anyone wants it?"

A spare place.

I was speaking before I even had a chance to fully process what Damien had said.

"Yes, yes, I want it! I'll come with you, I'll come with you!"

"OK, cool, man."

And that was that – I had the spare place. I had, all of a sudden, gone from feeling frustrated and down with a three-day trek ahead of me, to elated that I could get a helicopter out immediately. The desire to get out as fast as possible was overwhelming.

"Are you sure it's going to work, getting me on the helicopter; are you sure?"

I was concerned – it all seemed too easy; would it be better just to keep on trudging down the valley with the others, rather than taking a risk and ending up stranded?

"It will work," he said.

I dared to dream of Kathmandu. I could be there tonight, rather than facing three days' trekking, discussing the same issues over and over again, reminding me of our collective failure.

"How do you know they can take me?" I asked.

The others listened in on the conversation, adding nothing. I didn't feel too bad about jumping to the head of the queue for the space in Damien's helicopter, nor did I feel they begrudged me my speaking out to claim it. I knew him best, and if the tables were turned, I felt sure that none of them would have turned down a chance of a helicopter flight out.

"It is my helicopter, so there will be space for you."

"I'm not Belgian; I'm not part of your team."

"It should be OK – don't worry, it should be OK."

Jeepers, I thought. Now I had time to reflect, it was not so easy a decision to make. Should I trek down with the others, or sit it out with Damien at Gorak Shep and hope there would be space on his helicopter, if it even turned up – helicopters were in very short supply. Anyway, shouldn't the helicopter be doing emergency work? Was it right to use a helicopter? I rationalised that there was no harm in my jumping in the chopper, as it was coming anyway for Damien, so I would not be depriving anybody more needy of it.

If the chopper pilot refused to take me, it would be late and it would be dark. I wouldn't be able to trek down the Khumbu Valley at that time; it would be too dangerous, if I got stranded out in the open. The temperature would drop; I had no camping gear. I wouldn't survive the night – shit!

"What the hell," I said to Damien, "I really want to get home."

I took a sip of lukewarm lemon tea – it never tasted so good.

Soon after, John, Paul and Louise got up to go. We said our farewells, but it felt like we were leaving at the end of a funeral reception; our faces were sad, expressing our sorrow one last time.

"We should find our bags," said Damien, as the door closed after the others.

Oh shit, my bag… I'd strapped it to the back of some yak up at Base Camp. It could be anywhere down the Khumbu Valley by now.

It was going down to Kathmandu and would be left with the expedition team there. I could just contact them afterwards and get them to send it on. There was no way I was going to find the correct yak; it would be like finding a needle in a haystack.

My bags were safe on the yak; it would be simple enough to get the expedition management team to send them on to me when I was at home in the UK.

Damien spent the next hour or so pulling over yaks as they passed and looking for his belongings. I sat and watched, keeping half an eye out for my own, but not really rating his chances.

"Jules! I've got it!"

He dragged a huge, brightly coloured kit bag off the back of a yak, a big grin spread across his face. I clapped my gloved hands.

"Very impressive!" I said. "Now we just need the helicopter!"

Our spirits were reasonably high as we sat in the lodge waiting for our ride to arrive.

An hour passed. No helicopter.

Two hours passed. Damien rang again. Nothing turned up.

This wasn't looking good.

Slowly, as we waited, we became silent, staring at the phone on the table, praying for it to ring, or for some news – any news.

At some point, I had to make a decision whether to stay there or to pack it in and head on down to Pheriche to catch up with my expedition. It was a three-hour trek and I might end up doing the last part in the dark.

Damien rang again. His face lit up.

" 'Alf an hour!" he said, as he hung up. "They will be half an hour – it is all gud."

My heart lifted slightly. I dared to dream of Kathmandu again.

We had some more soup to pass the time, staring out over the courtyard at the mound of stones that acted as a helipad.

Time crept by as if it, too, was struggling with the altitude.

Suddenly, I thought I heard something, a constant, quick thumping in the distance. It grew louder, unmistakable – the sound of helicopter blades.

Damien and I rushed over to the door of the rickety hut. The helicopter, an anachronism of shiny metal against the ancient stone of Gorak Shep, whistled over the buildings and levelled out, preparing to land on the stone mound.

A Nepalese woman pulled on my sleeve.

"I go with you?"

I looked at Damien, who shrugged.

"Yes, OK," I said, smiling ruefully.

The wind from the blades battered us with cold but refreshing air.

I looked up at the helicopter hovering above. It was a little chopper with a large glass dome at the front. I could see the pilot's feet through the glass. It was so tiny I wondered where the three of us were going to fit.

The helicopter hit the ground and the door swung open. There were two seats at the front for the pilots, with a two-seater bench very close behind. The pilot remained in his seat, focused ahead – the engine was still running.

The three of us rushed forwards, crouching almost double, and jumped aboard. We shut the door behind us, shutting out the roaring sounds of the wind and the blades.

I couldn't quite believe that the helicopter was real.

The pilot turned around. He had two plastic tubes shoved up his nose. For a second I thought he was ill, flying our plane at death's door. I followed the tubes with my eyes and saw that they were attached to canisters under his seat.

Oxygen.

It made sense – these guys were flying up and down the Khumbu Valley on a daily basis, the changes in altitude were pretty bad for them, and the last thing they wanted was to become light-headed while in the air, so they hooked themselves up to oxygen cylinders.

The helicopter started to lift, dipping forwards slightly as it did. We were off!

But wait...something didn't seem quite right... The helicopter seemed to be labouring, unable to take off properly.

I felt it land back down on the stone helipad.

The pilot turned and shouted.

Oh shit, we're too heavy; he's going to kick me out. I'm going to be stuck here after all.

I strained to hear what he was saying.

"Bags! Out!"

Damien flung the door open.

"We come back, we come back!" the pilot shouted.

At that point, I didn't really care if they came back or not. I chucked my rucksack, containing my laptop – which is one of my most precious items – warm clothing and all of my electrical items, onto the stones below. I didn't care. I just wanted to get the hell out of there. Damien launched his bag out after mine.

The pilot shut the door again.

This time, the helicopter rose higher, dipping forwards before banking sharply right and heading down the Khumbu

Valley in the direction of Kathmandu.

I glanced up towards Everest, the imposing figure that had towered above me constantly for the past five or six weeks. I felt oddly numb as I looked at her peak one final time.

The helicopter turned so that I couldn't see the mountain any more, and for that I was thankful.

Fifteen minutes later, the helicopter swung down and landed in Pheriche – it would have taken three hours to trek all that way; we'd shot down like a rocket.

"I thought we were going straight to Kathmandu?" I shouted to Damien over the whir of the propellers.

"Me too!" he shouted back, shooting me a quizzical look.

"Everybody out!" shouted the pilot.

"Are we going further, what's happening?" I asked.

"Yes, yes, I come back, I get bags," he said without turning.

We jumped out of the helicopter, followed closely by the Nepalese lady, and ran clear of the blades. The helicopter lurched suddenly into the air and headed back up the valley.

Damien and I exchanged a look.

"Is this because of the thin air?" I asked.

"It must be."

The air was so thin up at Gorak Shep that the helicopter couldn't fly with a large load – it couldn't physically lift off. The air was much less thin down here – I could already feel it as I breathed in – so we would be able to take our luggage with us...after he went back and picked it all up.

I went to a nearby lodge to grab some drinks while Damien waited for the helicopter.

As I entered the building, I saw Donat and Iwan seated inside, having just trekked, like finely tuned Polish rockets, the three hours down the valley. They were way ahead of the rest of the expedition team.

"Hey Jules! How it going man?" said Iwan when he spotted me.

"Yeah, good," I responded cheerfully.

"Where is everyone else?" asked Donat.

"Still walking down the valley – I got a helicopter ride."

"Hey you lucky fucking bastard!"

There was a hunger in their eyes to get away; I'd seen the same look in the faces of Louise, John, Paul, all the rest. I strongly suspected I had that same mad glint in my own eye.

We shook hands, exchanged email addresses and I headed back to Damien, who was standing in the middle of the semi-dry riverbed next to the makeshift helipad. As I left the building, I could hear them shouting after me: "You lucky fucking bastard, we want helicopter, too!"

I arrived back at the pile of rocks as the helicopter was touching down once more. I could see a pile of bags in the back.

A Nepalese man approached us.

"I fly?"

He did not speak much English, but what the hell...the more the merrier! It was going to be a tight squeeze. The helicopter was a four-seater, but with all the bags and kit, there was barely enough space for the pilot and the three of us – me, Damien and the Nepalese woman.

We opened the door and were faced by a near impenetrable wall of kit bags.

"Everyone in!" shouted the pilot.

I clambered aboard, climbing on top of the bags, wedging myself in with my head stuck up against the ceiling. As long as I was on the helicopter, I didn't care how uncomfortable I was.

"This is cosy," said a voice near my right ear.

I craned my neck and saw Damien, wedged in an awkward position behind me.

"Beats trekking down the valley," I replied.

"Yeah, man!"

Once the four of us had somehow managed to squeeze ourselves aboard, the helicopter took off again. I spent the following 15 minutes staring at somebody's luggage, which was wedged in front of my face.

I felt us descending.

"Why are we stopping again?" I asked, my voice muffled by the bags.

"Refuel!" shouted the pilot.

There was a crunching noise, the sound of the helicopter landing on another rudimentary landing pad. The propellers died down and the door opened. I practically fell out of the helicopter, feeling slightly woozy from the journey.

I looked up, taking in my surroundings… Lukla. This was where my journey had really begun, the start of the ten-day trek, all those weeks ago, when I had flown here from Kathmandu at the start of the adventure. There was a small amount of damage from the earthquake – a few buildings had collapsed – but the short runway still jutted out into the valley like a nail, ending suddenly with an almighty drop.

"Are we not going to Kathmandu?" I asked the pilot, who had disconnected himself from his oxygen tube.

"Later, later," he replied. He took off again.

Damien and I walked away, towards the nearest lodge. There was a large sign hanging above the doorway that read 'coffee' and which drew us closer, like moths to a flame.

"Coffee and cake on me, if we can get it," I said.

"Stop! Stop!" shouted a female voice from behind us.

We turned to face the Nepalese woman who was hitching a ride with us.

"You stay," she said, pointing to where the helicopter landed. "You leave, you no get back on helicopter. You stay to get back on helicopter to Kathmandu."

I looked at Damien.

"I'll go and get us a couple of coffees and some cakes and bring them over," I said.

It was the least I could do – I was so grateful to Damien for getting me out of there, he could have asked for anything at that point.

I walked over to the lodge and bought two coffees in polystyrene cups – there were no cakes. I took them back to Damien at the helipad.

After 30 minutes, the helicopter returned.

The pilot jumped out and topped up the petrol from a jerrycan before beckoning to everybody to jump aboard. I jumped in, followed closely by Damien. The bags were now in the lockers in the tail of the chopper, and we were joined inside by two French trekkers.

The chopper took off and we flew the last 30 minutes to Kathmandu. I looked out of the window at the devastation below. As we flew over more built-up areas, I could see collapsed buildings, people running around like ants... The sun occasionally reflected blindingly on shattered glass in the streets.

Soon, we were flying over Kathmandu itself. The city was awash with activity; cars, people, bikes milling in the streets. Many of the newer buildings seemed to have escaped without serious damage, but some of the more ancient structures had been utterly destroyed. I could see people crawling over rubble, digging frantically at bricks. The sound of sirens, the sound of blaring horns, was everywhere.

As we descended towards the airport, I could see the location where once the monolithic Dharahara Tower had stood. Now, the sky was empty. The monument had collapsed, leaving only a stump like a felled tree; it was surrounded by white rubble that seemed like a thousand tiny headstones.

"Shit," I said, exchanging a look with Damien. There weren't many other words to describe it.

The helicopter touched down for the final time at the exact spot that I had taken off from nearly six weeks previously. We climbed out.

"What now?" asked Damien.

His question was answered when an open-backed truck screeched to a halt next to us.

"Passports?" said the driver. We showed them to him. "Jump in."

Why not?

We jumped into the open back and the truck lurched off, weaving through a chaos of planes and traffic. We drove around the perimeter of the hectic airport for nearly two kilometres.

I could see hundreds of large crates being hauled off cargo planes by men in military gear. I assumed it must have been foreign aid from around the globe. I could see the Indian military, the Chinese and the Americans – you could tell the Americans from a mile off; huge, barrel-chested men with the biggest helicopters, barking orders at anybody and everybody careless enough to stray within range.

We arrived at the terminal, the truck skidding to a halt, almost causing us to fall off.

"Out! Out!"

We jumped out of the back of the truck, which immediately shot off again and whistled around the corner.

We were left on our own, so we wandered through to the car park, completely ignored by everybody. No one gave us a second glance as they ran around in the chaos. It didn't seem as if anybody was really in charge.

"I'll get a cab," I said to Damien, flagging down the nearest one. We jumped in, slamming the door shut behind us.

The taxi driver looked back at us expectantly.

"Where to?" I asked Damien.

"I was staying in Thamel, but I don't think there's much left there now."

"Let's go there. If it's too bad, you can come back to the Hyatt with me."

The driver shot off in the direction of Thamel. It felt surreal; travelling in a taxi in a city that had just suffered a major disaster. As we tore through the winding streets, we could see the impact of the earthquake. Some roads were completely covered in rubble, forcing the driver to take detours. There were people everywhere, none of whom seemed to have any real purpose. It was chaos, utter chaos. The blare of sirens, horns and people shouting was incessant.

Eventually, we arrived in Thamel, at Damien's hotel. The area hadn't been as badly hit as we had been led to believe by the news reports, and the hotel was still standing.

He got out of the taxi and grabbed his bag from the boot.

"Look," I said to him, through the open window, "I really appreciate everything you've done for me."

"No problem, man – I just can't wait to crash out!"

We exchanged details, shook hands and he headed off into his hotel.

The Hyatt looked much as it had done when I had last seen it. The ornate gates still stood proud, and guards still patrolled the entrance. There were now lots of tents pitched on the hotel lawns, however. I knew there was a housing shortage in Kathmandu as a result of the earthquake, with many people forced to sleep in tents.

I paid the taxi driver and headed into the hotel, praying they would have a room for me, a proper bed that I could sleep in. I didn't really rate my chances – there had just been an earthquake, the country was in turmoil. Were they likely to have a spare bed? If not, I thought, I'll ask if I can sleep on the conference room floor. That would be far better than the freezing coffin tent I'd called home for the past few weeks.

I was hoping not to run into any of the others – I wanted to get out of the country as soon as possible, I wanted to avoid all the questions about the chopper, all the talk of our failure. I didn't want to have all the same discussions we'd already had. I was done, absolutely done with it. All I wanted was to get back home to see my precious daughters.

I walked into the foyer, expecting to see collapsed walls, gaping holes in the ground, some sort of indication that there had been an earthquake. Staff were busy filling cracks in the plaster, and a large crack had formed in the marble of the stairs, exposing the metal framework beneath, but on the whole, the building was remarkably intact, remarkably *normal*.

"Hello," I said to the receptionist. "I know it's a disaster area, but please, please, please, can you find me a room? I don't mind where, I don't care if it's the conference room... anywhere I can sleep."

"We've got a room for you sir; not a problem."

I could have hugged her.

She gave me a key card and I headed to my room – not my tent, not my coffin, my *room*. I pushed the key card into the door and opened it.

It was like going from the ridiculous to the sublime. I stood in the doorway, not quite able to believe my eyes. If somebody had told me this room existed in a city that had just been struck by a natural disaster, I probably would have laughed.

We had heard rumours of a water crisis in Kathmandu. But this room had air conditioning, an en suite bathroom with a lovely hot shower, a huge double bed, plasma TV, coffee-making facilities. It didn't seem real.

I walked in tentatively, as if the whole thing were some dream. I half expected to wake up, shivering in my coffin at Base Camp, hearing the eerie screams of the physiotherapist.

I felt guilty, too... With all this devastation around me, with thousands of people dead in Kathmandu, being in this swanky hotel felt kind of wrong.

But there I was. So I dropped my rucksack on the floor, stripped off and jumped straight into the shower. I scrubbed every inch of my body, and washed my hair, twice, three times.

I felt vaguely human again, but then I realised I had absolutely nothing to wear except the smelly gear I had just taken off – not even a clean pair of underpants.

Reluctantly, I climbed back into the same old clothes, and went in search of food.

The receptionist told me the buffet downstairs was open. "It's the only restaurant we have open, as we're short on staff."

Short on staff – the exact phrasing of this sentence sounded ominous.

As I walked down the stairs, it felt as if I was floating. It was so effortless after BC. My body, acclimatised for altitude, was now absorbing a huge amount of oxygen with every breath.

When I saw the buffet I couldn't quite believe my eyes. The opulence of the spread actually struck me as quite outrageous.

There were salads, pastas, hot and cold meats, noodles, fresh fruit, fish, roast pork...

I helped myself to a plate of food and sat down at a small table in the corner. My eyes proved bigger than my stomach, which must have shrunk from my time at high altitude. Altitude causes appetite loss; I practically had to force-feed myself at times at BC. I looked around at the people in the restaurant – almost exclusively Westerners – tucking into this food as though nothing had happened eight days ago.

I got chatting to a couple at the table next to mine. They were charity workers, just arrived to help distribute food up the valley to places devastated by the earthquake. Their presence in this expensive, lavish hotel seemed ironic to me – I found myself wondering how much of the charity pot was spent on their board and lodging. I was sure they were good people, trying to do the right thing, but they were just used to – and expected – their Western comforts.

After dinner, I went back to my room, stripped off and slept for what seemed like years.

* * * * *

I awoke the following morning with a throbbing headache. It seemed coming down from altitude was as bad as going up.

Where was I?

I opened bleary eyes and took in my surroundings. Realisation dawned on me delightedly – this was not BC.

I grabbed my phone from where it had been charging (what

a luxury – no flaky solar power!). I had emailed Vicky, updating her on my whereabouts in Kathmandu and begging her to find me a flight out. I rang her to see how it was going.

"I've got you a flight tomorrow," she said.

I was almost speechless.

"Tomorrow? Tomorrow as in Tuesday?"

"Yes! Tuesday, tomorrow!"

"You're an absolute saint! I cannot believe it. I just... Thank you so much!"

"I've got you on a Qatar flight. You fly to Doha and then back to the UK – you've got an eight-hour stopover," she said.

"That's brilliant! Amazing. Thank you so much."

I couldn't stop thanking her. I was overjoyed to be going home so quickly.

After the call, I still couldn't quite believe it; I was now truly desperate to get home. The Hyatt was very comfortable, but I had no reason to be there any more, no motivation and no goal. I just wanted to go home to my daughters.

I also felt out of sorts. My mouth was very dry, I kept sipping water constantly, and I was peeing like mad. My bladder felt full the entire time. My body clearly wasn't coping particularly well with the readjustment to a lower altitude. I thought you only suffered on the way up, but it appears that coming down too quickly also screws you up, though, fortunately, without any risk of brain embolisms!

I wandered outside, down the Hyatt's long drive and across the cracked road to the supermarket, to pick up some fresh clothes, and some small gifts for Steph and Lizzie. Housed in a large, modern concrete building with four floors, it was not obviously damaged by the earthquake, although, as I entered, I noticed a giant crack running through the middle of the broad central staircase.

In England, the shop would have been classified as unsafe, and closed – but here, they just got on with it. Security had been upped, with a security guard on each floor – I imagine there was huge concern about looters.

I grabbed some new underpants, socks and a t-shirt, and then found a silk scarf and a handbag each for Steph and Lizzie.

I spent the evening in the hotel bar with Hilary, who was already back. It was nice to see a friendly face, and it wasn't as bad as I had feared to be discussing all our recent adventures once more.

* * * * *

The following day, I was terribly nervous that, somehow, I wouldn't be on the flight list. I was convinced something would go wrong and I'd be stranded in Nepal – it all felt too quick and too good to be true.

I walked into the airport with my stomach in knots. I was sure there would be some sort of problem; some reason I couldn't get home to see my girls.

Even after I was checked in, with my ticket in my hand and a huge flood of relief surging through me, even once I was sitting in the plane, ready for take off, still I felt a strange fear that

I wouldn't be able to leave – that some higher power might prevent the plane from flying, or have me thrown off it.

But, finally, we were airborne... I was away.

I sat back in my seat and closed my eyes, drifting off to sleep for I don't know how long.

"Would you like anything to drink, sir?"

I opened my eyes and looked up at the sweetly smiling face of an air hostess, neatly dressed but with her hat slightly askew.

"What have you got?"

Epilogue: to the summit

It was November 2015 and I could feel the sweat on my palms; I was nauseous with concentration. All around me was still, but my head was spinning, and everything was topsy-turvy inside. I had to decide: next year or the one after. You see, the Nepalese government had agreed we could use our permits again for the following two years – so, in 2016 or 2017.

Earlier in the year 22 people had died, I had narrowly escaped death, and here I was thinking about going again. I could go in 2016, or in 2017, or, of course, not go at all. But what if I became ill again and couldn't go in 2017? It would be better to go now. But then I might die earlier, so maybe I should have another precious year with Steph and Lizzie... Round and round my thoughts went chasing each other.

I also wondered if being at EBC again, going through the whole process again, would bring back all the emotions from the 2015 experience. How would I feel? Would I arrive at EBC and immediately want to leave because of all the bad memories? There are deeper emotional reaches of the brain, which, when touched, can react so strongly that it becomes very difficult to keep a hold on reason. Given what I had witnessed in 2015, there was every chance that being back at

Base Camp would trigger things in me I might not be able to control. So I just didn't know if I should go.

Oh man, I just needed to make a damned decision. I emailed my good mate Damien:"Ho, Damien. Any good ideas?"

"Wow mate, I am very jealous, I cannot go this year – no cash – but try the Nepalese Asian Trekking expedition guys. They are very good, and Dawa Stephens, their head man, is half-Belgian, half-Sherpa."

I rang this company and spoke to Dawa. He seemed a very straightforward guy. They had a place on the expedition and he was happy to take me, so I signed up. Crikey, this was it; I was off again.

I headed out at the start of April 2016, checking in at the Yak and Yeti in Kathmandu – a great hotel, within walking distance of Thamel, the tourist area where all the climbing shops are.

Two days later we flew to Lukla, then trekked up the Khumbu Valley. The team was a good mixed bunch: Polish, Australian, Danish, Belgian, Indian, French, Welsh, myself – and Dr Nima, our expedition leader, a Sherpa and a qualified doctor – a great combination.

I made good friends with Christof, one of the Belgians. He was back for the third attempt. Another guy was back for his fourth attempt. This gave me some comfort in my moments of doubt. If they were coming back yet again, then surely I could manage it.

We arrived at EBC. It was bloody freezing, and I really, truly wasn't looking forward to my first night in the "coffin" tent.

"The tents are down there – help yourself; pick any one," said a Sherpa. I wandered down and picked the one at the end close to the WC – I never want to be too far away when the need arises and it's 3am and -15°C; that's one of the most miserable experiences in the world.

I crawled into the tent and, surprise, surprise, it was slightly bigger than last year. It was still a two-man coffin tent but slightly wider in the middle AND with a solar-powered light hanging from the tent wires in the middle – wow! Believe me, when facing six weeks sleeping in that coffin, even these slight improvements were a huge boost for my morale.

On the first night, I hung back in the mess tent as long as I could and, at around 11pm, I wandered down the hill to my coffin for the first time. It was eerily still, and I could see moonlight bouncing off the seracs across the glacial river running next to EBC. As it flickered spookily, I wondered about those lost souls from last year. Were they still here, seeking eternal rest? Were they waiting to welcome us into their unique club perhaps?

I crawled into my coffin, slid the Nalgene bottles into my sleeping bag, took off my thick thermal trousers and jacket and slipped into my bag – bloody hell, it was cold. My head, with its beanie hat, was pushing against one end of the tent and my feet the other. I lay there for a long time, staring at the plumes of steam coming out of my mouth with every breath; this was going to be an interesting night...

The next thing I knew somebody was banging the tent. "Jules, come on, it's breakfast!" It was Christof. That was the first night at EBC done, and I felt far better.

The Nepalese expeditions don't use Lobuche, they acclimatise on Everest. Fantastic – we would be on the big mountain straight away. I was really excited when, after 10 days at EBC, we got the call to make our first rotation up Everest herself. I remembered with vivid clarity the Icefall from last year, and how I had almost made it to the football pitch. Would I be able to get past it this time?

We rose at 1am. It was freezing cold, pitch black and every fibre in my body was tingling nervously; this was it. I had to empty my bowels. After bolting down some grub in the mess tent, I was off. I trudged through the icy wastes, the light from my head torch flickering against the glistening snow, towards the SPCC tent and the foot of the Icefall.

I arrived, fastened on my crampons, clipped in the jumar and up, up, up I went. The sun was now rising and I could see the full beauty of the majestic Khumbu Valley below me. The excitement was incomparable, along with my mad panting for oxygen – Jeepers, the air is so thin up there.

On and on I climbed, now in full daylight and out of breath. I turned a corner and stopped. Two of the guys with me had chest infections and could go no further. They decided to go back, but I wanted to carry on – so Tahar, Lakpa (one of the Sherpas) and I carried on. I was desperate to reach the football pitch.

We carried on climbing for another 45 minutes up one side of a crevasse and down the other, up another and down the other side. It felt as if we just weren't getting any higher. The sun was now beating down on the bottom of the Icefall. I was ready to go on, but with the sun melting the ice, the decision was taken to turn back. We were just short of the elusive football pitch again.

A week later I did another rotation and made it to Camp 1 – that was really hard. The last part of the Icefall is a 12-metre vertical wall of solid ice, and you have to haul yourself up. Then it's another half kilometre across the valley to Camp 1. I was absolutely shattered on arrival, and wondered how I was ever going to get any higher. We stayed at Camp 1 overnight, then returned to EBC.

With every rotation it got easier, so now the Icefall felt like a gruelling assault course rather than the end of the world, but I knew I could do it in about three and a half hours, so I timed everything, hoping to improve each time. I also counted the number of steps between each breath. It was generally four breaths for every step – not exactly quick going – and I was one of the faster ones.

Then, a week later, it was Camp 2, with two nights' rest and a climb to Camp 3 for a cup of Her Maj's finest before descending to Camp 2 for the night, and then back to Base Camp.

Finally, it was time for the real thing. Four of us were chosen by Dr Nima to make the first assault on the summit. There was a clear weather window of three days for us to get from EBC to the summit and back down to Camp 2 before the weather closed in. The air is so thin that helicopters cannot fly above Camp 2, so any mistake above Camp 2, and you stay where you fall in the snow for eternity.

I started my assault on the summit on Wednesday 11 May at 1am. And I reached it on Friday 13 May 2016 at 9.49am, spending a blissful 30 minutes above the clouds on the summit of the world.

For those 30 minutes I was the highest mountain in the world.

About Eye Books

Eye Books is a small independent publisher that passionately believes the more you put into life the more you get out of it.

It publishes stories that show ordinary people can and do achieve extraordinary things.

Its books celebrate "living" rather than merely existing.

It is committed to ethical publishing and tries to minimise its carbon footprint in the manufacturing and distribution of its books.

www.eye-books.com

About Extraordinary Things Done by Ordinary People

Other titles from Eye Books

Baghdad Business School, by Heyrick Bond Gunning
An account of the challenges, characters, comedy and catastrophe of starting up a logistics company in one of the world's most volatile regions: post-Saddam Iraq.
ISBN: 978-1-78563-021-7   £9.99

Good Morning Afghanistan, by Waseem Mahmood, OBE
"'I like you because you tell fewer lies than the rest.' For me that was a higher accolade than any MTV award; it was the trust of our audience." The true and compassionate story of setting up a radio station in post-Taliban Kabul, which helped earn the author an OBE.
ISBN: 978-1-78563-024-8   £8.99

Junkie Buddha, by Diane Esguerra
A mother loses her beloved son to a heroin overdose, but chooses not to be broken by it. Instead, she takes on the challenge of travelling to Machu Picchu to scatter his ashes there. This is a story about profound loss leading to spiritual gain. And it's a story about love.
ISBN: 978-1-90307-099-4   £8.99

The Mind Thief, by Maria Katsonis
This is the powerful and moving true-life story of a high-flying Harvard graduate who fought a terrifying battle against depression and psychosis. *The Mind Thief* will make you laugh, cry, gasp and smile. Written with elegance and honesty, it is a harrowing account of a complete mental breakdown, but is ultimately uplifting.
ISBN: 978-1-78563-019-4   £9.99

Riding the Outlaw Trail, by Simon Casson and Richard Adamson
"An adventure that suggests there's still plenty of "wild" left in the West. Exciting, uncomfortable and unpredictable." – *Wanderlust*
Inspired by *Butch Cassidy and the Sundance Kid*, Simon Casson and Richard Adamson (RIP) ride the trail of their boyhood heroes.
ISBN: 978-1-90307-065-9   £7.99

Jasmine and Arnica, by Nicola Naylor
This is the inspiring account of a unique journey. Told with a vivid and evocative insight, *Jasmine & Arnica* is a story of a young blind woman's determination, a celebration of the power of vision, beyond sight, to reveal what's closest to the heart, and to uncover life's most precious, unseen joys.
ISBN: 978-1-90307-076-5   £7.99

Walking Back to Happiness, by Christine Palmer
Slightly overweight, pale and discontented, Christine begins her journey from southern France to Santiago de Compostela in northern Spain on a quest to fit into a deliciously skimpy silk Bellino top.
ISBN: 978-1-90307-069-7   £7.99

Moods of Future Joys, by Alastair Humphreys
Thunder and Sunshine, by Alastair Humphreys
At the age of 24, Alastair Humphreys set off to try to cycle round the world. By the time he arrived back home, four years later, he had ridden 46,000 miles across five continents, on a tiny budget of just £7,000. *Moods of Future Joys* takes him through Europe and the length of Africa. *Thunder and Sunshine* takes him home via the Americas and Asia.
ISBN: 978-1-90307-085-7   £7.99
ISBN: 978-1-90307-088-8   £7.99

Squirting Milk at Chameleons, by Simon Fenton
Chasing Hornbills, by Simon Fenton

"Much more than *A Year in Provence* goes to Africa." More like "*No.1 Ladies Detective Agency* meets *Driving over Lemons*."

Simon Fenton leaves Britain in search of adventure, and finds Senegal, love, fatherhood, witch doctors – and a perfect piece of land for a guest house, if only he knew how to build one.

ISBN: 978-1-90307-091-8   £7.99
ISBN: 978-1-78563-026-2   £8.99

Green Oranges on Lion Mountain, by Emily Joy

Emily Joy puts on her rose-tinted specs, leaves behind her comfortable middle class life as a doctor in York, and heads off for two years' voluntary work at a remote hospital in Sierra Leone. She finds the prospect of life in a rural African village less than enticing. There is no equipment, no water, no electricity and, worst of all, no chocolate to treat her nasty case of unrequited love.

ISBN: 978-1-90307-073-4   £7.99

For more information about these and all of our titles, please visit www.eye-books.com